D1025118

BANNER OF PEOPLE'S WAR,
THE PARTY'S MILITARY LINE

GENERAL VO NGUYEN GIAP

Banner of People's War, the Party's Military Line

Preface by Jean Lacouture
Introduction by Georges Boudarel

PRAEGER PUBLISHERS
New York • *Washington* • *London*

PRAEGER PUBLISHERS
111 Fourth Avenue, New York, N.Y. 10003, U.S.A.
5, Cromwell Place, London S.W.7, England

Published in the United States of America in 1970
by Praeger Publishers, Inc.

© 1970 by Praeger Publishers, Inc.

Library of Congress Catalog Card Number: 72–120153

Printed in the United States of America

Contents

Banner of People's War, the Party's Military Line

Preface

by

JEAN LACOUTURE

When I was invited to write an introduction to this book, I asked my friend Georges Boudarel if he would like to make it a joint undertaking. Of all the scholars I know, he is the best equipped to explain Vietnamese strategic thought. His long sojourn among the revolutionaries in the Vietnamese forests and ricefields has provided him with unique experience and a knowledge, both intuitive and rational, of the military thinking of Hanoi's leaders.

To his illuminating introduction, I should merely like to add some personal memories, so that readers may have some sense of the man who is the commander in chief of Vietnam's People's Army when they read Giap's dense and stiff prose, which is so typical of the writings of military activists.

It was on February 3, 1946, that I met Vo Nguyen Giap for the first time. He was then Minister of the Interior in Ho Chi Minh's second government, which had been formed after the elections of the preceding month—elections in which the Viet Minh had defeated the nationalist, anti-Communist parties. These political parties were, nevertheless, well represented in Ho's government. What role had Giap played in the victory of his comrades? Had he used force to ensure their success? He was said to be very authoritarian and rather insensitive to customary demucratic procedures.

The man I saw come into the reception room of the former official residence of the French governor of Tonkin, where he met me, was quite slight in build, a little stooped, and with a head that was too large for his body. His round face was notable for its huge, Beethoven-like forehead, thick lips, and, particularly, the liveliness and intensity of the expression in his slightly protruding eyes. It was a striking face—that of a poet or a Roman orator—and a disturbing one in the passion it expressed: This was not a person who could be easily swayed or who could be readily persuaded to abandon his objectives.

His conversation was as interesting as his appearance. He was typical of those emotional Vietnamese (who are far less impassive than legend admits), with a dash of romanticism and a smile concealing either great suffering or great irony.

He was regarded then as Ho Chi Minh's most faithful disciple, and he was even closer to Ho than Pham Van Dong was. During this period of conquest, he carried major responsibilities—as Minister of the Interior—prior to his appointment as Minister of Defense when the time came to resume the war with France.

In February, 1946, negotiations were under way in Paris between the Viet Minh and the French Government. Ho Chi Minh and Jean Sainteny were meeting secretly every day, and the French negotiator was only waiting for the green light from Paris and from the High Commissioner in Saigon before concluding what became, a month later, "The March Sixth Agreements."

We talked about these negotiations. Giap spoke of independence, the *doc lap,* as an absolute necessity, without which, he said, the Viet Minh would resume the war. "We shall not let ourselves be stopped by any loss, any violence, any destruction," he interjected with a force that made a strong impression on me. This man was not just a politician, a gambler, or an opportunist. He was clearly a fighter of immense energy. But he also knew how to moderate his words, and never in the course of that conversation did he exclude the possibility of an understanding with France.

On the evening of March 6, the day the agreements were signed, I saw Giap again at the villa of Ho Chi Minh, and then again on March 18 at the same place, when Ho received General Leclerc, who had arrived in Haiphong the day before with the agreement of the Viet Minh authorities. The meeting between the old Communist leader and the intrepid French officer, whom everything should have separated and who hit it off immediately, seemed to fascinate Giap. In a low voice, he said to me, "So everything may be possible, after all."

A month later, Giap was head of the Viet Minh delegation that met with the French at Dalat—a meeting that paved the way for the Fontainbleau Conference. There he demonstrated impressive eloquence in denouncing the war that the French Expeditionary Corps was then conducting in Nam Bo (the south). His disputes with his counterpart, Pierre Messmer, who later became de Gaulle's Minister of Defense, were extremely harsh.

The evening of the day the meeting ended, Giap granted me a long interview. He then insisted on rereading its entire text, correcting it with the care of one who loves the French language, which he speaks to perfection. It was he who suggested that I use the term *le désaccord cordial* to describe the Dalat Conference. His political intelligence—and his intransigency—informed each sentence. He was a rough, vehement, and provocative speaker. No other Vietnamese has made such a strong impression on me, not even Ho Chi Minh or Pham Van Dong.

That was the last time I saw Giap. Three months later, he became Defense Minister. Six months later, he had a good deal to do with the hardening of the Viet Minh attitude toward the French troops at Haiphong and played an important part in Hanoi's decision to adopt a strategy of rupture with the French. For the next seven years, he was the commander of Vietnam's red army, crowning his campaign with the devastating victory at Dien Bien Phu.

On my first visit to Hanoi after the war, in 1961, I naturally asked to see General Giap, along with Ho Chi Minh and Pham Van Dong. Giap was the only one whom I was unable to meet: He was, so they said, "convalescing" at Don Son on Along Bay. In fact, his political position was a very difficult one at that time. In 1956 and 1957, he had been the chief critic of the "dogmatism" of Truong Chinh, the leader of the pro-Chinese wing of the Party. Four years later, his boldness was to cost him dearly, for Peking's star was rising in Hanoi.

Since then, the man whose friends once called him "the volcano under the snow," to portray the mixture of fiery intensity and cold determination that is his strength, has resumed his place in the Party's top leadership and has reinforced his position as strategist, chief of the armed forces, and heir to and disciple of "Uncle Ho." Too marked by his campaigns against the "dogmatists" to be acceptable to Peking as a candidate for Ho's succession, too strongly influenced by Vietnamese nationalism to be a Party leader in the full sense of the term, Giap is one of the most powerful incarnations of revolution—social and patriotic, romantic and scientific, totalitarian—in the name of a kind of liberty. An Asiatic Castro controlled by a Stalinist structure?

Giap is the very opposite of a finicky, pedantic bureaucrat. For a man sixty years of age, this disciple of Ho's is extraordinarily vigorous, impassioned, and colorful, with flashing eyes and animated gestures, and a voice that is sometimes dramatic and sometimes droll.

Beyond all the arid prescriptions for the perfect revolutionary fighter, or the dry, hygienic recipes of the works of Mao or Che Guevara, we must try to catch a glimpse of the revolutionary as a man. With Giap, we must picture his genius and his passion. Thanks to Georges Boudarel, Giap's "thought in uniform" is much more understandable. But under the uniform is a small man with the head of a lion and the brow of a thinker, a man who has used revolutionary violence as the terrible raw material for the building of a nation. Yet, because Ho and Giap have extracted their country's independence at a great cost, Vietnam will survive and may one day gain the civil rights that will transform it into a free society.

Introduction

by

GEORGES BOUDAREL

In Giap's writings, certain phrases recur like a musical theme. One, in particular, embodies the others: *our experience*. In this expression, the adjective counts as much as the noun. The didactic tone should not mislead us; Giap's ideas, far from being abstract, are the fruit of practice—a practice that is captured in the title of his first theoretical essay for the general public, which he wrote in 1960: "The Great Experiences Gained by Our Party in Leading the Armed Struggle and Building Revolutionary Armed Forces." [1]

Before 1939, the Communist Party of Indochina (CPI) had undergone two major tests: The first was the defense of the rural Nghe Tinh soviets (1930); the second was the united front in a primarily urban context during the Popular Front in Paris in 1936. If the first of those efforts recalls the Chinese soviets of Hailufeng in the 1920's, the second is, by contrast, rather close to that of the labor parties of the West. It was not until the World War II period that the lessons of those two movements were drawn. Then, while an underground movement operated in the delta and in the towns, a guerrilla base area was established at Cao Bang, in a region adjacent to the frontier with China. Although it was at first only a safe training center for Party cadres, the base area gradually extended its power—first into the villages and then to the districts—before resorting to armed struggle. When Giap left Cao Bang for the "march to the South" in 1943, he was less interested in liberating territory than in rapidly establishing a liaison between the two prongs of the Vietnamese revolution:

[1] See Vo Nguyen Giap, *People's War, People's Army* (New York: Praeger Publishers, 1962), pp. 65–150.

the rural and urban delta area, where about half of the Central Committee was located, and the Cao Bang base area, where the other half worked with Ho Chi Minh. When the Liberation Army was established on December 22, 1944, it was only a propaganda section of thirty-four men. But within six months it had spread like water, and by June, 1945, the whole northern region between Hanoi and Cao Bang had been transformed into a liberated area. The decisive struggle did not take place in the mountains, however, but in the towns. On August 19, while Giap's men were still fighting at Thai Nguyen, an uprising led to the overthrow of the pro-Japanese government. At the time, Party leaders explained their victory solely in terms of the thought of Lenin, Stalin, or Mao. Although the experience of the October Revolution had been grafted onto that of Yenan, the Vietnamese Revolution retained a distinctive identity of its own. A new experiment had just succeeded: a uniquely Vietnamese revolution. The cities had not been encircled from the countryside; they had exploded from within, of their own accord. Nevertheless, the seizure of power in the towns would not have been possible without the magnetic attraction and the enthusiasm inspired by the Cao Bang base area. At a given moment, either the rural or the urban sector could have played the dominant part, but, in the movement as a whole, neither one can be considered decisive. With time, the special character of the Vietnamese Revolution would become apparent—particularly in the military sphere.

As the war expanded after December, 1946, it revived another specifically national tradition—that of resistance. Villagers again began to make snares and dig traps. In response to the course of French search-and-clear campaigns, certain villages spontaneously transformed themselves into fortresses by digging a whole network of tunnels. Several major offensives were named after heroes of Vietnamese history: Lê Loi, Tran Huong Dao, Phan Dinh Phung, Ly Thuong Kiet, Quang Trung.

The great wars of Vietnamese history have never really involved complicated professional maneuvers where, to cite Clausewitz, "Time and Chance shuffled the cards." [2] Since the tenth century, under a centralized government, military recruitment has been carried out under regulations that approximate conscription. Total war, which was unknown in Europe prior to 1792, has been the strategy of all great Vietnamese military leaders when confronted by an invader. They did not hesitate to appeal to the people to meet the threat with widespread guerrilla warfare, optimal use of the terrain, and campaigns in which highly mobile units carried out surprise attacks on the enemy. In the Hanoi Museum today, one can see one of the stakes that Tran Huong Dao had his men plant in the Bach Dang riverbed as a trap for the Mongol ships. By pretending a frantic flight upstream, the Vietnamese drew the Mongol ships into the river at high tide. As the tide ebbed, the ships were impaled on the stakes and could be boarded. Alongside that exhibit are the earthenware vessels that Vietnamese implanted in their roads to break the legs of the enemy's horses. The memory of that distant past was kept alive by the long resistance of the rebels led by Phan Dinh Phung in 1885–95 and by Hoang Hoa Tham, who roamed the forests near Hanoi until 1913. A 1914 novel by Phan Boi Chau [3] suggests how vivid the memory remained. Indeed, it is hard to say whether his novel is a historical narrative or a prophetic work. It tells how a partisan leader opens a "mountain road" within an ethnic minority area so that it can serve as the backbone of a great resistance movement and can parallel the coastal road along the border, which is held by the Chinese. Repeating the exploit of one of the Tay Son brothers, he captures a fortified town by having his own

[2] General Carl von Clausewitz, *On War,* translated by Colonel J. J. Graham, new and revised edition, with introduction and notes by Colonel F. N. Mavda, C. B. (late R. E.), III (London: Routledge & Kegan Paul, 1962), 97.

[3] Phan Boi Chau, *Hau Tran Zat Su* (in Chinese) (*The Extraordinary History of the Later Tran,* Hangchow, 1921), translated into Vietnamese by Tran Le Huu (Hanoi: Van Hoa, 1957).

soldiers, disguised as mandarin couriers, bring him into town in a cage.[4] Under the noses of the enemy, some women keep inns that serve as centers for recruitment and espionage; others open commercial establishments to smuggle goods between the free zone and the occupied zone. In this novel about the fifteenth century, one can almost perceive the news stories of today about the Ho Chi Minh Trail or the Tet offensive.

General Tran Hung Dao condensed his strategy in an excellent formula: "Defeat the greater with the lesser." Because today's revolutionaries are fighting on the same territory, they have become aware that they are applying the principles of that traditional strategy. This is not surprising. Lenin owed his military ideas to Engels and Clausewitz, who had drawn theirs from Royalist Spain's guerrilla war again Napoleon. Mao grew up on Lenin and Sun Tzu. The military history of Vietnam is surely a match for that of Spain. All of Vietnam's ancient strategists had studied Sun Tzu.[5] Without discounting his own abilities, Giap today can place his entire career in the direct line of the historic generals of his own country. He has affirmed this more clearly than ever since 1967, particularly in his statement of December, 1969, which should be subtitled: "A Brief Summary of the Military Art of Vietnam." It may well seem paradoxical that his re-examination of a distant past should appear at a time when Vietnam is locked in a struggle with the West's most modern army. But, then, it was while meditating on the deep thrusts of the Mongol cavalry that Basil Liddell-Hart clarified his ideas on armored warfare tactics. Giap proceeds in the same way, but his perspective is different. He looks at the Mongol campaigns from the point of view of the people whose country was invaded, rather than from that of the invader.

[4] Giap's first military operation was similar. On December 22, 1944, with thirty-four men dressed as partisans, he seized the post of Phai Khat in a surprise attack. His men entered by the main gate. He carried out the same stratagem the next day at Nang An. The present repeats the past—even in anecdote.

[5] It is significant that Sun Tzu, *The Art of War,* was translated from Chinese into Vietnamese by the People's Army Press in 1964 (Quach Hoa Nhuoc, trans., *Binh Phap Ton Tu*).

The massive American intervention that began in 1965 posed military problems for the National Liberation Front and the Democratic Republic of Vietnam that no other national liberation movement had ever had to resolve, and the problems were subjected to intense discussion. A similar debate in 1954 at Dien Bien Phu had involved the choice between either a massive and rapid assault on Dien Bien Phu or a slow erosion of its points of support. By 1965, however, the debate focused not on the principle of people's war but on how it should be conducted; not on the necessity of resistance, but on the forms such resistance should take.

Although the available information does not permit any detailed conclusions, it is possible to discern two distinct approaches in the Vietnamese texts of the late 1960's. The first was articulated by General Nguyen Chi Thanh, who died in Hanoi in the summer of 1967. He placed more stress on the need for an offensive response to the American buildup, but he made no concrete analysis of the military situation. His writings concentrate on political and moral ideas and discuss them from a very broad point of view. In spirit, they are much closer to Lin Piao's statements of recent years than to those of Mao Tse-tung during his campaigns. That spirit has been captured in this highly voluntaristic formula: "During a revolutionary war, the revolutionary theory and line in themselves contain a vast potential for an uninterrupted supply to the revolutionary war of the material forces necessary to overthrow the material forces of the enemy." [6]

By contrast, Giap's approach is characterized by a much stronger awareness of the situation. For him, the human element interacts with natural forces that act upon man; politics are based on the current demands of each day; military action is dominated by man's will but also by improvements in his technical level. Giap regards the offensive as imperative, even in the defensive phase. But even more important to him than

[6] Nguyen Chi Thanh, in *Visions of Victory: Selected Communist Writings, 1964–1968,* with an analytical introduction by Patrick J. McGarvey (Stanford, Calif.: Hoover Institution, 1969), p. 64.

the offensive itself is its central thrust, its point of impact, and its potential for strengthening the revolutionary forces.

However great the difference may have been between Thanh and Giap, it does not seem to have seriously affected the conduct of operations. In 1965, the only superiority that the Vietnamese could claim in relation to the enemy, and thus their only source of strength, was their will to win. With their potential for resistance, they countered the saturation bombing of their territory by mobilizing their entire people for the fight against the American planes and counterattacked American units in hand-to-hand engagements. Furthermore, the initially divergent points of view of Giap and Thanh were reconciled in practice. The NLF forces remained in their positions and took the offensive in direct attacks on newly arrived American units. There was no pure and simple return to guerrilla warfare, nor was there any retreat to the mountains, although those possibilities seem to have been considered. The practical solution corresponded to the spirit of Nguyen Chi Thanh's speeches. The North has provided the South with both logistical and operational support, but without having to commit the major part of its forces or endanger its reserves, the preservation of which is the essential condition for carrying out the protracted war. The use of the North as a great rear base area, whose purpose was to serve as a sanctuary and source of reserves throughout the hostilities, certainly accords with Giap's statements.

At the same time, military operations underlined the importance of new problems that Mao Tse-tung had not had to face during his campaigns in China: the devastating effect of American firepower on a very small country, the emergence of important logistical needs in the revolutionary camp, the impact of warfare on the interaction between the cities and the countryside (artificial and rapid urbanization in the South, as a result of the American presence, the bombing of an industrializing rear area in the North and the dispersion of its industries), and the possible modernization of the revolutionary forces as a result of aid from the socialist countries.

(For Giap, the present war is a "war of local aggression whose level of conflict is scaled to the existence of a socialist rear base area.") [7]

It was under the influence of all these factors that the theories formulated here by Giap gradually took shape. While Nguyen Chi Thanh stressed almost exclusively the global and moral character of the relationship between the revolutionary and counterrevolutionary forces, Giap believed that the relationship should "not only be considered at the international level, but also in the context of a single sector, in the limited confines of South Vietnam." [8] Giap's revolutionary line is defined in terms of the smallness of the territory and its limited resources. Within that framework, military action should engage all the resources of the nation in every area and in every sphere—political, economic, cultural, diplomatic, and military. This struggle—"the combined strength of all revolutionary means" [9] and the total war of the entire people— is aimed simultaneously at military and political targets, guerrilla warfare and local insurrection, in order to unleash a general insurrection. Those operations that are strictly military are to be led simultaneously by three types of forces—regular, regional, and guerrilla. They are to receive support on three levels—moral, material, and tactical—through methods designed to heighten their political consciousness, provide the necessary equipment, and improve their combat tactics.

Although Giap's thinking seems at first glance to be a synthesis of Lenin and Mao, of Clausewitz and Sun Tzu, it is actually closer to the latter two than to the former two. Lenin conceded only a relative and transitory importance to guerrilla warfare. Giap, on the other hand, like Mao, conceives of it as an essential condition for revolutionary war, although he

[7] Vo Nguyen Giap, *Notre Guerre du Peuple A Vaincu la Guerre de Destruction Américaine* (Hanoi: Foreign Languages Publishing House, 1969), p. 42. Speech to the meeting of cadres of the Third Military Zone in July, 1969.

[8] Vo Nguyen Giap, *Le Peuple du Sud Vietnam Vaincra* (Hanoi: Foreign Languages Publishing House, 1965), p. 30. The Vietnamese text of July, 1964, was published in *Quan Doi Nhan Dan*.

[9] See p. 102 below.

does not go so far as to say that all power emerges from the barrel of a gun, or that the countryside encircles the cities. In considering recourse to various forms of revolutionary violence, Giap diverges from Mao and returns to a "classic" Leninist line. Whereas Mao sees the entire revolutionary process as a war that emerges from guerrilla warfare, Giap conceives of the process as a more complex one, in which both the legal and the illegal struggle within the existing political structure have important roles to play in the revolution. Although Giap never stated the paradox openly, his reasoning is based on a principle of the economy of means, which was concisely stated by Sun Tzu: "To subdue the enemy without fighting is the acme of skill." [10] Giap's entire strategy is designed to exploit the interaction between the concentration of the enemy's forces and the space in which the revolutionary forces can move. By sending all available men into the countryside, he seals it against the enemy and extends the elusive front of guerrilla warfare in every direction. Concealing his own strengths, he marks his enemy's weak points, and then strikes in order to slip through enemy lines. His art contains Sun Tzu's stratagems. Yet, because this people's war is fought against the West, it gives the impression of having assumed a more Western character. It is the "organic whole" whose "center of gravity" Clausewitz sought to ascertain so that he could attack it with the concentrated blow of all his forces. [11] Thus, the military line evolves as hostilities develop. "Each style of warfare," Giap writes, "must be adapted to the balance of forces between the enemy and ourselves and to the strategic situation of each phase of the war." [12] The problem is not to win this or that battle but to select the form of combat that will prove most rewarding at the strategic level. The points to attack will vary according to different purposes. Depending on the phase of the war, the emphasis may be military or

[10] Sun Tzu, *The Art of War,* translated and with an introduction by Samuel B. Griffith, with a foreword by B. Liddell-Hart (Oxford: The Clarendon Press, 1963), p. 77.
[11] Clausewitz, *op. cit.,* Vol. III, 125.
[12] See p. 89 below.

political, or even both at once. But in the final analysis, politics remains the ultimate objective and the key to all action, because "the strength of the revolutionary war is the centralized manifestation of the all-out strength of the revolution." [13]

Without putting it in so many words, Giap's new strategy is protracted war, which is designed to counter the deployment of the American military machine in a country whose resources are limited. He does not refer to the theory of the three-phase war, derived from Mao, which Truong Chinh developed in 1947 in his *The Resistance Will Win,* but instead draws on the experience of the August Revolution to support a new theory. In the new conception, the counter-offensive phase becomes a general insurrection with simultaneous political and military action. Attacks on the enemy's base areas take precedence and, in a sense, the enemy's rear becomes the main front. The fact that the countryside and the mountainous areas constitute the principal base of support for the revolutionaries does not make them the revolutionaries' center of gravity, since, depending on circumstances, this center may be located in the towns or in the countryside. Actually, in Giap's formula of the three strategic sectors, the front is everywhere at once, in the mountainous areas as well as in rural areas (plains and river delta) and the towns. For Giap, all three strategic sectors are of equal importance.

At the same time, the consolidation of base areas on three levels—in mountainous areas within the South, the socialist rear area in the North, and the rear provided by the entire socialist camp—has a greater strategic impact than ever before in preparing for insurrection. It is here that technical modernization can play a significant role, for Giap does not overlook the fact that it is possible to win battles in a relatively short time by taking advantage of all favorable conditions.[14]

This task of scientifically organizing people's war has pro-

[13] See p. 26 below.
[14] See p. 68 below.

found implications for operational tactics. It corresponds to the advance from the bow and arrow to the machine gun. The fighter passes from the age of the bamboo spear and the trap into the age of the transistor and the rocket. The specifically military aspects of warfare henceforth assume far greater importance than in Chinese Communist theory, where human will is the only key to all solutions.[15] Although Giap believes that man's will ultimately prevails, he recognizes that, at a given moment, military technology may play the dominant role in a particular situation. "Redness" does not resolve all problems by the immanent grace of magic formulas. Military action is dependent on the strength of an army's firepower. It demands "rationally organized and equipped elite forces with the capacity to meet the demands of different methods of warfare." [16] If man is decisive, then "arms and equipment are the material and technical base of combat armies, the basic element of their strength." [17] Thus, the greatest importance will be attached to new arms, whether it is a question of planes, anti-aircraft, radar, or rockets.

There can be no contradiction between the tactics of and strategy for protracted war, since a successful strategy emerges from successful tactics. An operation makes sense only in the degree to which it strengthens the revolutionary camp—an ancient principle of guerrilla warfare. By constantly increasing their combat effectiveness, a smaller force should be able to concentrate its regular forces to launch an attack against and overcome a larger and more mobile enemy. This is an-

[15] From this point of view, Giap's ideas are closer to Che Guevara's concept of a guerrilla elite than to Mao's theories. Similarly, the August Revolution more closely resembles the Cuban Revolution (as represented by the Sierra Maestra rebel stronghold in combination with the internal crumbling of the Havana regime) than the massive and purely military offensive of Mao in 1949. The Vietnamese conception of the launching of a guerrilla movement is nevertheless very different from that of the Cubans. For the Vietnamese, the guerrilla movement always starts with a peasant type of self-defense (as in China), while, in the Cuban *"foco"* formula, an outside force intervenes in order to instigate a military movement and then undertakes to create a political movement. The Vietnamese process is just the opposite: Initially political, it becomes military.

[16] Giap, *Notre Guerre du Peuple A Vaincu la Guerre de Destruction Américaine,* p. 30.

[17] See p. 36 below.

other application of the "few against many" principle, of which Vietnamese history offers many examples. Although Giap does not regard it as an inflexible rule, that principle replaces Mao's theory that victory in combat requires absolute numerical superiority.

To carry out the highly technical operations of the new type of "people's war," Giap has created "the method of independent fighting by the crack special units, whose numbers are small, but whose quality is high." [18] These small, highly mobile groups, composed primarily of various types of brilliant specialists and armed with excellent equipment and artillery, lead constant attacks on the enemy's bases. Although the elite units had been in existence for some time, they were first mentioned officially in September, 1967. Several months later, they became the spearhead of the Tet offensive.

In battle, the size of the units, the degree of concentration of forces, and the element of surprise play a critical role. Even if the battle of Dien Bien Phu could be classified among the outdated types of warfare discussed by Giap (and this is doubtful), we would still do well to remember the surprise role that artillery played in that battle, as we seek to gain a better understanding of Giap's present intentions, particuarly when he speaks of surprise attack.

In the final analysis, people's war, as Giap conceives of it, is a war prolonged by the maximum economy of forces. In conducting people's war, the aim is to gain time. It follows that every operation must produce an increase in strength. According to that theory, the extension of war in time is obtained by the brevity of military actions and by limitations on the number of troops participating in attacks on points selected for their shock value. Although total war is of a highly technical nature, it remains a people's war; although it requires the general and diversified participation of the population, that is not its sole prerequisite.

What are Giap's objectives for the immediate future? The

[18] Vo Nguyen Giap, *Big Victory, Great Task* (New York: Praeger Publishers, 1968), p. 69.

answer is both all and none—all in that he intends to exert equal pressure in every sphere; none in that, for a certain period, he will regroup his forces in order to make a new qualitative leap forward in the military struggle. At present, he accords equal priority to political and military action. All forces must join together to bring about the encirclement of the enemy, even in his rear areas, and to prevent the enemy from fully using his power. By taking a sentence out of context here or there, Giap can be made to say that he favors a return to primarily political action and that he means to transform the political climate in the towns.

This hypothesis is not altogether baseless. The outlook from Saigon is not exactly encouraging, to cite, for example, reports about the Song My massacre, various scandals among the Green Berets, and the sentencing of Deputy Tran Ngoc Chau to ten years of hard labor, despite his appeal to President Nixon. Moreover, the Huynh Van Trong affair [19] demonstrates the pervasive character of relations between the insurgents and the government.

That kind of climate creates a very favorable environment for contacts of all kinds. The National Liberation Front, the only organization with solid roots among the people even when its presence is not generally visible, may be in the process of gaining some government collaboration, much as the Viet Minh did in 1945, when it won the cooperation of such top officials as the imperial delegate Phan Ke Toai, now Vice Premier in Hanoi, who transferred power to the Viet Minh. In his references to the August Revolution in December, Giap was certainly aware of such a prospect.

[19] Huynh Van Trong, special assistant to President Nguyen Van Thieu, was condemned on November 29, 1969 to life imprisonment at hard labor for "high treason." His case was handled as an emergency ruling, without right of appeal. Some sixty individuals, suspected of having maintained contacts with the National Liberation Front, were implicated in the case. Following the trial, three of the accused were condemned to life imprisonment at hard labor, and thirty-seven others to terms ranging from three months of prison, with a suspension of the penalty, to twenty years at hard labor. (See *Le Monde* and *Le Figaro,* July 30, 1969 and December 2, 1969.) In reporting the affair, the press recalled the "Green Berets incident," in regard to the murder of a Vietnamese civilian on June 20, 1969. (See *Le Monde,* August 13 and 14, 1969.)

At the same time, Giap realized that the Communists had been able to recruit some of their opponents in 1945 only because a vast popular uprising had been supported by a dynamic guerrilla movement. Thus, to consider only one side of Giap's thought would be to misrepresent his views. For Giap, there is an important interaction between the ripening of the political situation and the pressure of insurrection. His method is to play all the cards in his hand; that is his strength, and it would be surprising if he were willing to limit his options. For him, victory is not to push the Americans into the sea but to destroy their plan to "Vietnamize" the war. One salient of his strategy is aimed at the cities; the other two remain directed toward the populous rural areas and the vast operational zone of the mountains.

Even if certain types of operations are likely to be abandoned (most probably those that permit the U.S. Air Force to intervene with maximum effect), we would be deluding ourselves to foresee any decrease in the military action of the Democratic Republic of Vietnam and of the Provisional Revolutionary Government of South Vietnam, since their position has been strengthened by the strategic blow delivered against the Pentagon during the Tet offensive of 1968. Although the tactical success of that operation is debatable, there is no doubt that the process of American withdrawal originated then, and that it operates in favor of the insurrection. Moreover, the discontinuation of the bombing of the North creates an essential condition for the conduct of protracted war; both the North and the South can increase the military potential of their revolutionary forces—a situation that may hold some future surprises. Like Mao, Giap has always regarded the possession of a sanctuary as the essential condition for the conduct of the war. All of Giap's recent statements suggest that he is actively strengthening his firepower and that specific agreements have been concluded with the socialist countries to that effect. The unusual space accorded to socialist aid in Giap's December, 1969, statement [20] confirms this impression: This was not the case several years ago.

[20] See p. 55 below.

By raising the level of its regular troops and militia to that
of the regular forces, as regards both equipment and training,
the Democratic Republic of Vietnam is now organizing masses
of reserves that it never had before. On several occasions in
the past, Giap has noted the lack of anti-aircraft rockets that
could strike American planes at their bases in South Vietnam.[21] The Soviet Union has given such arms to the United
Arab Republic. Is it inconceivable that it might do as much
for Vietnam one day? The American forces would then lose
their principal trump card. The importance that the Hanoi
press has attached for some time to everything involving the
Soviet Union and Stalin's anniversary in December, 1969,
suggests that the possibility cannot be disregarded.

At the same time, the American position has continued to
deteriorate despite such tactical successes as the recovery of
the Plaine des Jarres in Laos in the fall of 1969—a Pyrrhic
victory, as it turned out. In South Vietnam, one can only be
skeptical about the Vietnamization of the war—this return to
the "special war" whose catastrophic failure is at the root of
the 1965–69 "build-up." Faced with the impossibility of
launching an offensive of the traditional kind, the Pentagon
increasingly conceives of the conflict as an industrial undertaking, with saturation bombing and the spraying of de-
foliants, which disrupt the entire ecology of the country.

Since the Song My affair, the most unlikely people have
become concerned about the way land operations are being
conducted. Such harsh methods of warfare carry serious political risks for the United States: They have even elicited opposition within government circles in Saigon to the American
presence. Even the purely military effectiveness of massive air
raids is highly doubtful. In March, 1970, although American
B-52's were forced to withdraw temporarily from raids in the

[21] "To fight enemy aircraft and to battle his ground forces are two quite
different things, especially when we lack a powerful air force and long-
range missiles that are capable of destroying enemy aircraft at their bases
or even at a certain distance from their targets." From the report of Vo
Nguyen Giap to the cadres of the Third Military Zone in July, 1969. The
French text appeared in *Le Courrier du Vietnam*, August 13, 1969, and in
Vo Nguyen Giap, *Notre Guerre du Peuple A Vaincu la Guere de Destruction Américaine, op. cit.*, p. 48.

South in order to concentrate their bombing on northern Laos, they were unable to prevent the fall of the Plaine des Jarres, which controls access to Vientiane and Luang Prabang.

At present, when chances for obtaining reinforcements are limited by the political situation in Washington, the adventuristic activities of the CIA outside of Vietnam serve only to increase the weaknesses of American forces by diverting them into blind alleys.

The events since the coup d'état of General Lon Nol at Phnom Penh on March 18 and the intervention of American troops in Cambodia on April 29, 1970, illustrate once again the effectiveness of Giap's strategy in operating on the scale of the three eastern countries of the Indochinese peninsula. In response to the late April operation that was to capture the supreme headquarters of the National Liberation Front and advance the "Vietnamization" of the war, the resistance forces shifted the axis of their operations in two directions: outward toward the rural zones and inward toward the core urban areas. Their action took both a military and a semilegal form.

Within a month, almost the entire countryside in Cambodia had been lost by the government formed after the coup d'état. As of the beginning of June, the Communists had sufficiently established themselves in the western regions of the country so as to take action at Angkor Wat and Siemreap. At almost the same time, the Pathet Lao crossed the frontier into Saravane.

In South Vietnam, Communist troops attacked thirteen points in the city of Dalat on May 30 and then disappeared after having suffered almost no losses. For the first time, an operation of this sort had been launched entirely from the interior, evidence of a significant strengthening of the clandestine military networks since the Tet offensive of 1968. In Saigon, the most diverse opposition forces demonstrated in public, particularly in the student and Buddhist circles that had been so active prior to the fall of Ngo Dinh Diem in 1963.

Since April 29, the insoluble military problems that the Pentagon has faced in South Vietnam have been extended to the two neighboring countries. The second Vietnam war has become the second Indochina war. Today, however, Prince Sihanouk, who has hardly been known for his extremist opinions, finds himself at the head of the insurgents organized by the Cambodian left.

By extending the conflict into the rest of Indochina, the United States is sealing its own fate. How can one forget that Giap's victory at Dien Bien Phu was made possible by his brilliant maneuvers in 1953–54 across the three countries of the Indochinese peninsula?

Conditions are thus favorable for the intensification of the political and military efforts that Giap anticipates. It is likely that an element of surprise, with both political and military implications will erupt during the course of diverse and simultaneous campaigns in the mountains, the delta, and the cities. At that point, an attack on key points by limited military forces could lead to that final turn in the war about which Ho Chi Minh was dreaming when he composed his poem on chess in a Kuomintang prison in 1943:

Eyes must look far ahead, and thoughts be deeply
   pondered.
Be bold and unremitting in attack.
Give the wrong command, and two chariots are rendered
   useless.
Come the right moment, a pawn can bring you victory.[22]

On the Vietnamese chessboard, two great games were won by that strategy in 1945 and 1954. Although the revolutionaries lack the major pieces, they are the only ones with any real freedom to maneuver throughout Vietnam. In the third match, now under way, the National Liberation Front and the Provisional Revolutionary Government have more pieces on the board than Ho's team had fifteen years ago.

[22] *Ho Chi Minh on Revolution: Selected Writings, 1920–66,* edited with an Introduction by Bernard B. Fall. (New York: Praeger Publishers, 1967), p. 136.

BANNER OF PEOPLE'S WAR,
THE PARTY'S MILITARY LINE

This year, we are enthusiastically celebrating the twenty-fifth anniversary of the founding of our Vietnam People's Army (VPA) and are preparing to celebrate the fortieth anniversary of the founding of our great Party. With fervent revolutionary spirit, all our armed forces and people, in both the north and south, are resolutely striving to implement President Ho's historic will.

The south, the fatherland's great, heroic front line, is staging simultaneous attacks and uprisings, with great victories. Proud of our achievements in protecting and building socialism, the north is wholeheartedly fulfilling the duties of the great rear base area toward our brothers in the south.

Under the glorious banner of our Party and great leader Ho Chi Minh our people have struggled over the past forty years, scoring great victories along the national liberation path, opening a new era—the era of the fatherland's independence and freedom and of socialism in our country—and making worthy contributions to the world's revolutionary undertaking.

Born and raised in the people's revolutionary tide and enjoying the Party's clear-sighted leadership, Uncle Ho's solicitous care, and the people's wholehearted assistance, our People's Army has developed from nothing into a great, powerful, heroic, and indomitable revolutionary force endowed with a tradition of glorious victory. This is due, above all, to our people's and armed forces' possessing an invincible weapon: our Party's Marxist political and military line.

As an organic part of its political line, a creative application to our country's actual circumstances of the Marxist-Leninist doctrine on war and the army, and a recapitulation of the many practical experiences afforded by the uprising of all the people and people's war of the Vietnamese revolution, our Party's military line has inherited, developed, and improved to a new level our nation's age-old traditional stategic ability. At the same time, it has selected and accepted the experiences of the world revolution's advanced military struggle. In the past, at present, and in the future, this line has remained and will continue as an ever victorious banner of our armed forces and people. On these historic anniversaries, let us direct our attention to our Party's military, revolutionary, and scientific line and advance toward defeating U.S. aggression completely.

PART 1. *The Successful People's War Against [the Foreign Invader], Our People's Revolutionary Struggle for National Salvation, Independence, and Freedom Opened the Road for Vietnamese Society to Move Toward Socialism, and It Is a Continuation of Our Nation's Heroic, Several-Thousand-Year-Long Struggle to Defend and Build the Country. Our Party's Military Line in This Revolutionary Struggle Is Not Separated from Our Nation's Long-Standing Military Tradition.*

Because of its important geographical position in Southeast Asia, our country, since its founding by King Hung, has had continually to rise up to struggle against invading forces. The process of this struggle is going on at present, thus making our people's history an epic full of many heroic feats of arms in the fight against aggression, to safeguard the nation's existence and the fatherland's independence and freedom.

From the beginning of [the first century B.C.] to the eighteenth century, our people waged more than twenty fierce, nationwide wars to liberate the country or to safeguard national sovereignty.

During a thousand years under the foreign feudalist yoke, our people rose up again and again to regain national independence, beginning with the Trung sisters' heroic and successful nationwide revolt and including the national liberation uprisings and wars under the leadership of the Ly Bon and Mai Thuc Loan dynasties. Finally, Ngo Quyen's glorious victory on Bach Dang River in A.D. 938 ended the ten-century-long period of foreign domination and opened a long period of independence and self-government for our people. Since then, throughout nearly a thousand years of independence, we have had to conduct many wars to protect our country from foreign aggression in order to safeguard our national sovereignty.

These wars were: the resistance under the Ly Dynasty, with

the determined and bold offensive conducted by Ly Thuong
Kiet, who first took the initiative in frustrating the enemy's
onslaught and later counterattacked and annihilated the Sung
troops on Nhu Nguyet River, thus dooming their aggression;
the resistance under the Tran Dynasty in the thirteenth century—the most symbolic resistance—which, under Tran
Huong Dao's command, three times over a period of thirty
years defeated the aggressive army of the Mongolian horde
who, although famous for their cruelty and combat efficiency
and having repeatedly won from Asia to Europe and con-
quered nearly half the world, were brought to complete defeat
in Thanh Long; the Lam Son uprising, under the leadership
of Le Loi and Nguyen Trai, which was turned into a ten-year-
long stanch and persevering national liberation war and which
finally ousted the Ming army from the country and restored
independence after twenty years of foreign domination; and
the resistance under Nguyen Hue—based on the new strength
of the widespread revolutionary movement of the peasants,
who rose up and fought successfully against feudalism and
corruption in the country—a resistance later turned into a
war of national defense that, through lightning operations,
within seven to eight days. annihilated 200,000 Manchu
troops, thus dooming the last aggressive war conducted by
foreign feudalism in our country.

Generally speaking, these popular uprisings and national
liberation wars were led by a feudal class, but all of them were
obviously people's wars, in which our people voluntarily played
the active role in rising up and fighting together for national
salvation. It can be said that these uprisings and wars were of
popular character in our country.

Through this long and continuous struggle, our people's
intelligent and valiant military tradition was shaped. It accumulated and developed our ancestors' rich strategic knowledge.

In modern times, in the middle of the nineteenth century,
the French colonialists began invading our country. Despite
the Nguyen Dynasty's cowardly surrender, our people val-

iantly rose throughout the country and waged resistance wars led, successively, by Trung Cong Dinh, Nguyen Trung Truc, and so forth, in the south, and by Phan Dinh Phung, Nguyen Thien Thuat, Hoang Hoa Tham, and so forth, in the north. It took the French imperialists some thirty years to occupy our country. Later, their rule was continuously shaken.

In the old days, our people had permanently to face aggression by great foreign powers that, like our country, were under feudal regimes. There was only a slight difference between their economic, cultural, and technical levels and ours. But now we have to face a war of colonialist aggression waged by a capitalist power far superior to us not only in numbers but also in economy, techniques, equipment, and ammunition. Our Party was born to shoulder the historical task of leading the Vietnamese revolution in this new era of mankind, a transitional period from capitalism to socialism on a world-wide scale, initially marked by the great October Revolution in Russia.

Under these historical circumstances, our Party, headed by President Ho, the Vietnamese Communist who first creatively applied Marxism-Leninism to the actual circumstances of our country, set forth a correct revolutionary line—a people's democratic national revolutionary line toward socialist revolution, [bypassing the] capitalist development phase. Our Party has led the advance of the national liberation struggle along a completely new path.

With its correct political lines, which were set forth at the outset in the 1930 political programs, our Party succeeded, in the process of its revolutionary leadership, in mobilizing the extremely large revolutionary forces of the working class and the peasants—the basic forces of the national, democratic revolution—and in building a steady worker-peasant alliance bloc under leadership of the working class, using it as a basis for the [formation of a] broad, united national front.

The Party's military lines were shaped on the basis of these correct political lines, and they have been gradually improved through the realities of our people's protracted revolutionary struggle. From the very beginning of our Party, a revolutionary storm of the masses has swept through the country, its height being the 1930–31 Nghe-Tinh* Soviet movement. For the first time in our country, the peasants' movement was closely combined with that of the workers; the worker-peasant alliance was achieved, and the [the Party's] sole right to leadership over the working class, which has been represented by our Party, was asserted in practice. Under the leadership of the Party's regional chapters, the workers and peasants in Nghe An and Ha Tinh arose and conducted uprisings and used revolutionary violence, thus combining political and armed struggles in order to topple the regional colonialist rulers, officials, and villains and to set up worker-peasant administrations in a number of rural areas.

Later, in the 1936–39 democratic movement, our Party cleverly combined the overt, legal, semi-overt, and semi-legal struggles with secret and illegal activities and started a vigorous movement of political struggle in the cities and rural areas, to oppose colonialist reactionaries and the feudalistic king-official clique, to demand freedom, democracy, and a better life, to oppose aggressive fascism, and to protect world peace.

This building of political forces and launching of the political-struggle movement constituted a basis for advancing toward the era of new revolutionary struggle that followed. During World War II, our Party, faced with a new situation, asserted that the national liberation task was its main one and that it considered the preparation for an uprising of central importance at that time. The Party founded the united national front in order to muster all forces on a broad basis.

Under the Party's leadership, the masses' revolutionary movement proceeded from political struggle toward armed struggle and from the masses' political organizations toward the building of revolutionary armed organizations. It cleverly combined the political and armed struggles, started local

* Short for Nghe An and Ha Tinh provinces.—ED.

guerrilla warfare and a partial uprising, brought revolutionary fervor to its highest degree throughout the country, and moved toward a general uprising to seize the administration.

The August Revolution of 1945 was a general uprising of the entire population. In a short time, the revolutionary masses under the Party's leadership arose as one in the cities and the rural areas, in both the north and south, smashed the ruling yoke of the Japanese fascists and the pro-Japanese administration, seized the administration, and founded the Democratic Republic of Vietnam (DRV) throughout the country—the first people's democratic state in Southeast Asia. The August Revolution was the first success of Marxism-Leninism in a colonial and semi-feudal country. Our people had grasped an extremely favorable historical opportunity and, through armed uprising, had scored nationwide success.

From the revolutionary high tide of 1930–31 to the August Revolution of 1945—throughout the fifteen years of our people's brave struggle to seize the administration—our Party's military lines were basically shaped. Immediately after the success of the August Revolution, our people had to conduct a resistance against the French colonialists, who, aided by the U.S. interventionists, returned to our country and invaded it.

Our first sacred resistance lasted eight to nine years and was concluded with the great success in the 1953–54 winter-spring period, the climax of which was the historic Dien Bien Phu campaign. The victory caused the French colonialists to sign the Geneva agreements and to re-establish peace in Indochina on the basis of the signatory countries' recognition of the independence, sovereignty, unification, and territorial integrity of the Vietnamese, Khmer, and Laotian peoples. The northern part of our country was completely liberated.

This resistance was a continuation of the August Revolution, a national liberation war, and our people's war to defend the fatherland. This was the resistance of a small, underdeveloped agricultural country that defeated an aggressive

500,000-man professional army of an imperialist power much more powerful in equipment and technique and enjoying U.S. aid, which provided 80 per cent of war expenditures.

In this resistance, our people's very important support was the newly formed world socialist network. The success of our anti-French resistance was the first great victory in the war for the liberation of colonial peoples. In this resistance, our Party's military line was further developed and improved in every respect.

As soon as their first protracted resistance ended successfully, our people had to continue the struggle against U.S. imperialism, [which sought to replace] French colonialism in the aggression against the southern part of our country. The U.S. imperialists have plotted to turn the south into their neo-colony and military base from which to attack the north, to oppose the socialist camp, and to check revolutionary development in Southeast Asia.

This time, our country's aggressive enemy is none other than the United States, the most prosperous and powerful ringleader in the imperialist camp, which possesses impressive modern war machinery and great economic and military potential, is an international gendarme, and is the number-one enemy of all mankind.

Under the flag of the National Liberation Front of South Vietnam (NLF), the heroic South Vietnamese, standing fast at the forefront of the fatherland, have increased their already strong revolutionary zeal and have written glorious pages in the history of our nation.

In 1959–60, after several years of stalwart, fierce political struggle, a general revolt erupted in the vast rural areas of South Vietnam. This was a valiant and creative uprising of millions of our compatriots who, with the masses as their main political force and with a very small armed force, rose up to smash the enemy's oppressive yoke in villages and hamlets. Their aim—to wrest back control from an enemy possessing more than 200,000 troops and the apparatus to cause great oppression—the collapse of the fascist Ngo Dinh Diem regime.

The successful general uprising developed into a revolutionary war or a national liberation war against the U.S. special war waged by 500,000 puppet troops and more than 30,000 U.S. advisors who, in repressing the national liberation movement and counterattacking against the southern revolution, applied the latest experiences of international imperialism.

Our people have been conducting the second sacred resistance against aggressive U.S. imperialism. In only four years, the heroic southern armed forces and people annihilated and eroded a great part of the puppet army and administration, defeating the U.S. puppets' strategic-hamlet state policy and basically foiling the U.S. imperialists' special war strategy.

Because U.S. imperialism has sent U.S. expeditionary and satellite troops *en masse* directly to invade the south and to wage a war of destruction against the north in order to avoid failing in the south, our armed forces and people throughout the nation have unanimously and resolutely risen, in response to President Ho's sacred appeal, to struggle to save the country from U.S. aggression, to liberate the south, protect the north, and proceed toward national reunification. This is a revolutionary war, a liberation war against the greatest, most brutal regional war in the history of U.S. imperialism, [a war] that has achieved a high escalation with more than 1 million U.S., puppet, and satellite troops, with several hundred billion dollars of war expenditures, and with modern weapons of all types, not including nuclear weapons.

With matchless gallantry, our people were determined to take the offensive. The more they fought, the more they won, and the stronger they became. Therefore, after only three years, the southern armed forces and people achieved the Mau Than spring general offensive and uprising, which created a turning point in the history of the war and forced the enemy to be on the defensive on all battlefields, tacitly to recognize the bankruptcy of their local war, and passively to adopt the de-Americanization or Vietnamization of the aggressive war.

The revolutionary war in South Vietnam has moved to a new phase, scoring greater and more comprehensive successes than ever before and proceeding toward complete victory. The southern revolution and revolutionary war are synthesizing, applying, and developing by one new step the experiences of the August Revolution, of the resistance against the French, and of all previous Vietnamese revolutions.

The northern armed forces' and people's struggle completely defeated the war of sabotage essentially perpetrated by modern U.S. air power, a people's land-air war never known before in our country. For the first time, we carried on a war of defense in the socialist north, making use of perfected state institutions to fight the invaders, to safeguard strongly the socialist north, and to fulfill the task of being our country's great base area.

We realized an entire people's war, coordinating resistance, strongly stepping up the people's air defense, resisting while continuing socialist building, fighting while producing, guaranteeing satisfactory transportation and communication, maintaining order, defeating all U.S. war escalations, thus completely defeating their war of sabotage after four years of valiant fighting.

Our nationwide resistance to the United States has been the greatest and the most glorious resistance to aggression in our people's history. It is the vanguard front and the apogee of the world's peoples' present common struggle against the U.S. imperialists. In this resistance, our Party's political line has been developed by one [more] step, with many rich experiences in many aspects. Under the Party's leadership, continuing our nation's indomitable tradition of struggle, our people have fought unremittingly for scores of years, have successively defeated the aggressive armies of three great imperialist countries, have actively contributed to the collapse of old colonialism, and have vigorously promoted the failure and bankruptcy of neo-colonialism in the world.

This justified President Ho's saying, "Our nation is a heroic nation; we defeated the Japanese fascists, the French colonialists, and are now determined to defeat the aggressive U.S. imperialists.* Our people may be proud to be one of the nations possessing the most valiant traditions of stanch struggle against aggression and imperialism."

* President Ho's appeal on July 20, 1965.—ANNOUNCER

PART 2. *The Entire Country Has Fought the Aggressors Under the Vanguard Party's Leadership.*

In the protracted fighting under the Party's leadership, our people have accumulated rich experiences in various respects. Regarding the enemy and his forms of aggressive war, our people have gained experience by using armed uprisings and revolutionary wars to defeat, successively, three great imperialist powers on three continents: the Japanese fascists—the cruel fascist in Asia—the French colonialists—a great colonialist power in Europe—and the imperialist United States—the top imperialist and an international gendarme. We have thwarted all their forms of aggressive war, from the old colonialist wars of aggression of the French colonialists and the Japanese fascists to the U.S. imperialists' neo-colonialist war of aggression, and from the U.S. neo-colonialist policy of ruling by fascist maneuvers through a puppet lackey administration to the U.S. special and local war of destruction by air force and navy.

Regarding methods of struggle and of using revolutionary violence to regain and preserve administrative power, liberate the nation, and defend the fatherland, we have become experienced in staging uprisings of all the people, uprisings in rural and urban areas, and partial and general uprisings throughout the country; in using armed struggle in a protracted war as a main instrument to oppose an old colonialist war of aggression; in waging people's war, revolutionary war against various forms of neo-colonialist war of aggression; in combining military struggle with political struggle, military offensives with uprisings in war; and in waging a people's ground-to-air war to defeat the U.S. war of destruction.

Regarding our conditions, our historical conditions at home and abroad, our people have gained experience in waging people's war, revolutionary war under greatly different historical conditions—sometimes not yet having a revolutionary administration, sometimes having assumed local or national powers, sometimes relying on the strength of the emerging people's democratic regime, sometimes relying on the superiority of the socialist regime under construction, sometimes applying throughout the country a unified revolutionary strategy (the people's democratic, national revolutionary strategy), sometimes practicing a different revolution for each part of the temporarily divided country, sometimes with a world war unfolding due to infighting among imperialists on a world-wide scale, sometimes rising and fighting a resistance war without a world war, sometimes, still immature and weak in strength, being obliged to fight a resistance war while being surrounded on all sides by imperialism, sometimes being able to rely steadily on the vast socialist camp, and so forth.

This situation has been reflected in the protracted, arduous, complicated, and violent character of our people's revolutionary struggle. Because of the extremely important strategic position of the Vietnamese revolution in Southeast Asia, the international imperialists—from the French to the Japanese, then the French again and the Americans and their satellites —for scores of years have intensively and continuously used counterrevolutionary violence to repress our people.

Faced with such strong and cruel enemies, our people, our nation, under the Party's glorious banner, have heightened their stalwart and unsubmissive spirit of resistance and their thoroughly revolutionary spirit in firmly maintaining and developing the offensive position of the revolution, in leading our country's revolutionary undertaking from victory to victory, in scoring marvelous achievements in our nation's history, and in making worthy contributions to the world revolution.

This situation has also been reflected in the very inspiring practical basis of the Party's revolutionary and military lines that require us to have a very high independent, self-governing and creative spirit, with which we cannot copy foreign experiences nor be complacent about the experiences we have acquired.

From these points, we can indicate the following basic characteristics of the war that our people have waged under our Party's leadership.

First: This is a just war, a national liberation war, or a war to protect the fatherland, aimed at implementing the Party's political line and at achieving revolutionary objectives for the sake of the people, the Vietnamese people, and the world revolutionary endeavor of opposing the unjust, aggressive war being waged by imperialism. War is a continuation of politics. Our Party's revolutionary lines decide the political objectives of the revolutionary war and the just nature of the war being waged by our people.

Conversely, the imperialists' colonialist, aggressive political lines decide the unjust, counterrevolutionary nature of their war. The military tradition of our forefathers and fathers was, in essence, the tradition of waging a just war to save and protect the country. For our people's survival and benefit, the feudalistic class that led the uprisings and national liberation wars in our history hoisted high the banner of a great cause, of saving the country and the people and of implementing various definite forms of democracy in an effort to achieve national unity and to save the country.

Although limited by the framework of the feudalistic regime, this military tradition has permeated the "great ideology of the just war aimed at protecting Vietnam," * the "policy urging the entire country to join in combat," the "policy of strengthening the people and of considering this the best means to protect the country," † and the "policy of using a great cause to doom cruelty and of using intelligence and kindness to doom violence." ‡ It is due to the goal of saving our country and race from national destruction that our people's just war has succeeded in mobilizing an invincible force, namely, our people's patriotism and unity.

In the present era, the national liberation revolution is an

* Ly Thuong Kiet.—GIAP
† Tran Huong Dao.—GIAP
‡ Nguyen Trai.—GIAP

inseparable component of the world proletarian revolution. Our Party's revolutionary lines have pointed out that the basic objectives of the revolution are national independence, people's democracy, and socialism. These basic objectives also constitute the political goals of the uprising and national liberation war, or war to protect the fatherland, that our people have conducted through various phases of development of the revolution.

Our present revolution and revolutionary war have closely combined the national liberation problem with the problem of the "people's struggle for the right to democracy," have closely combined the national liberation path with the socialistic path, and have closely combined the Vietnamese revolution with the world revolution.

President Ho said: "To save the country and liberate the people, there can be no other path than that of proletarian revolution." Our Party's national salvation banner has closely combined the national and class factors and the national and international factors. This has been reflected in the law governing the objective development of Vietnamese society in the present era. This has also been reflected in basic interests and deep aspirations of the working class and our laboring people and entire people, which are consistent with the interests of the world revolution. Therefore, with its just nature, the national liberation war or the war to protect the fatherland being waged by our people under our Party's leadership has acquired new content with regard to its quality and an entirely new strength.

Our just cause has vigorously mobilized the forces of our entire people and our entire country to stand up to fight resolutely, to liberate our people, and to protect our fatherland. The just cause and success of our revolutionary war have succeeded in mobilizing the support of the forces of the progressives all over the world. This constitutes our inexhaustible source of strength, which the enemy can never evaluate. This constitutes a basis for the absolute superiority of our Party's military lines.

Second: This is a national liberation war, a war to defend the fatherland of a people whose not very vast and populous country was a semi-feudalist colony with an underdeveloped economy and who, endowed with a long-standing anti-invasion tradition, are building a new regime—the people's democratic regime, the socialist regime.

This is a war of a brave, intelligent, stalwart, and resourceful people who use a small, weak army to fight and defeat the huge, strong, aggressive army of an imperial power whose vast and populous country has a great economic and military potential and modern technical equipment. Throughout the history of our people's anti-invasion wars, and at present, we have always had to struggle against invasion by powers with more vast and populous lands and a greater army. In previous epochs, however, these big, aggressive countries were under feudalist regimes, as was our country.

Nowadays, the aggressors are imperialist powers, which are far superior to us not only in numbers and superficialities but also in highly developed industries, great economic and military potentiality, and modern weapons.

Our country is not very vast or populous and was a semi-feudalist colony with an underdeveloped economy. However, unlike our ancestors, we are proceeding toward and becoming masters of a new socialistic regime—the people's democratic regime—a socialist regime that is definitely superior to the aggressor's reactionary and rotten one. We are endowed with the great strength of our progressive socialist regime and of today's Vietnamese who are mastering this regime.

From this comparison of strength, to win the present national liberation war, a war for safeguarding our fatherland, our people, in order to defeat the enemy, are relying on winning popularity and on taking advantage of terrain and opportunities for developing highly the new strength of the progressive socialistic regime and of the Vietnamese in the present epoch.

On this foundation, our people have carried on and developed to a new level our country's intelligent and valiant anti-invasion tradition, which had known not only how to use weakness to defeat strength and to use the few to defeat the many in new conditions, but also how to use civilization to defeat ruthlessness, how to use our definite superiority in political and spiritual strength to conquer the enemy's iron and steel, and how to combine modern weapons with relatively modern and rudimentary weapons to defeat the enemy's modern weapons.

On the basis of our people's determination to win, their sagacity and creativity, we have used our fundamental strength to limit and defeat the enemy's relative strength and to intensify the enemy's fundamental weaknesses, thus developing the full power of the people's war in the new era for attacking and defeating the enemy.

Third: This is a national liberation war, a war to defend the fatherland, that is being conducted in the extremely advantageous international conditions of the present era, an era of success for the socialist revolutions and those for national salvation, when revolutionary forces are stronger than anti-revolutionary forces on the international plan, and when world revolutions are on the offensive against imperialism.

In the old days, our fathers, struggling in the feudal era, had to rely completely on their own forces, for no one supported and assisted them. Nowadays, our people are carrying on the liberation war, a war to defend the fatherland, in completely different international conditions. The great success of the Russian October Revolution gave birth to a new era in the history of mankind, the era of capitalist ruin and of world-wide socialist victory. It united the working class's socialist revolutionary movements in developed capitalist countries with the oppressed nations' national liberation revolutionary movements.

The Vietnamese revolution led by our Party is an inseparable part of the world revolution and has won the collaboration and broad support of revolutionary movements in various countries, especially after World War II, when Soviet victory over the fascists created advantageous conditions for

successful revolutions in many European and Asiatic countries.
The world's system of socialist countries was born and has
become the decisive factor in the development of world revolutions. The socialist camp is the firm wall and [protective]
moat upon which nations can rely in their liberation struggles in the new era. With the success of the Chinese revolution and the foundation of the People's Republic of China,
the world's revolutionary forces—the core of which is the
socialist camp—became stronger than the anti-revolutionary
imperialist forces.

The world revolution is attacking imperialism continually
and from many directions and is achieving many great victories. This international situation is very advantageous to
the revolution and revolutionary war in Vietnam in the present epoch.

Today, our people are building and defending socialism in
the north. At the same time, they are undertaking the resistance to the United States, in order to liberate the south
and advance toward national unification. Our revolution has
reflected the association between the two revolutionary cur-
rents of our time—the socialist revolution and the national
liberation revolution. This is a very fundamental strong point.

It has strengthened the position of our revolution in the
world revolution. In the protracted and arduous struggle to
defeat the big and powerful imperialist aggressors, our people—with our Party's correct revolutionary line and correct
international solidarity line based on Marxism-Leninism and
proletarian internationalism—have been making positive contributions to the world revolution's common cause. Simultaneously, we have been receiving an increasingly large
amount of aid from the Soviet Union, China, and other fraternal socialist countries, and we have been enjoying active
support from the progressives, [an important] factor in the
success of the revolutionary war in our country.

As for the imperialist aggressors, they represent the reactionary social system that has been condemned by history.

They are endeavoring to regroup their forces, in frantic opposition to the attacks of the world revolution. However, along with other reactionary forces, the imperialists are being driven into an increasingly weakened, defensive, and defeated position. They are being opposed in increasingly strong measure by people in their own countries, and they are becoming isolated in the world. Their internal contradictions are becoming more and more fierce.

This is one of the fundamental weaknesses of today's imperialist aggressors. It is also a great advantage for our people's struggle. During the previous war of aggression against our country, the Japanese fascists were defeated by the Soviet Union and its allies. After having been defeated and having lost their country during World War II, the French colonialists rehabilitated themselves. Now the U.S. imperialists— leaders of imperialist camp—are encountering various difficulties and contradictions, are sustaining repeated defeats, and are declining.

These characteristics of our revolutionary war are deeply reflected in the content of our Party's military line. Our Party's military line is the people's war line. It originates from and is subservient to our Party's political line. It is the war line of the Vietnamese people who are struggling for national independence, people's democracy, and socialism.

Applying Marxist-Leninist views on revolutionary violence, our Party's military line has the following fundamental content: The entire country fights the enemy under the leadership of the working class, the fighting power of all the people is developed, and an uprising of all the people and people's war are launched to defeat the imperialists' large, aggressive forces.

Long ago, the founders of Marxism-Leninism spoke of people's war. Engels held in high esteem the French people's struggle during the 1793 bourgeois revolution, calling it a mass uprising, an uprising of all the people, a people's war. Engels also called the Chinese people's struggle against the

British colonialists in the mid-nineteenth century a people's war to preserve the Chinese nation and, in the last analysis, a genuine people's war.

In our country, we have the tradition of launching uprisings of all the people and people's war to liberate our nation and defend our territory. In our history, there has been anti-aggression people's war led by the feudal class, and people's war developing from the revolutionary movement launched by the Tay Son peasants against the country's corrupt feudalists and the aggressors from abroad. Now we have people's war led by the working class. Our people's war in the past—whether it derived from peasants' revolutionary movements or was led by the feudal class—had [historical] limitations [both in] its objectives and in the forces that led or undertook the war. Nowadays, our people's war, led by the working class, is a war fought by the people and for the people, with its fullest meaning and content in the new era.

The revolutionary lines of our Party—the representative of the Vietnamese working class—are aimed at achieving national independence, people's democracy, and socialism in our country. Our aim is to make our people's war most fully combine with the national goal of saving the people and with the liberation and protection of the fatherland through the working people's liberation. Therefore, basing their actions on our Party's political lines, the nationwide forces now fighting the aggressors are the most powerful and broadest of our people's entire forces that have ever stood up to fight.

Our Party has mobilized and organized the all-people unity block, joined in the broad, united national front, and used the worker-peasant alliance as a foundation for uniting closely with the working class under the working class's leadership, and with the people world-wide. This constitutes the new, invincible strength of people's war. Fully aware of their revolutionary task and the war goal, the forces all over the country that are now fighting the aggressors have the great strength of national consciousness and of Vietnamese patriotism and tradition along with the new aspects of the present era.

This is a patriotism united with the democratic spirit and love for socialism and proletarian internationalism. This is our people's ardent patriotism combined with the working class's thoroughly revolutionary spirit. With the new strength of the entire country now fighting today's aggressors, our people's war mainly relies on its own strength and fights the aggressors in our country with the strength of the Vietnamese people and the advanced socialist regime of Vietnam, while also leaning on the extremely large amount of support and aid from the world revolution, whose nucleus is the socialist camp.

Our military lines consist of creatively adopting the revolutionary-violence viewpoint of Marxism-Leninism, of considering revolution an undertaking of the masses, and of regarding revolutionary violence as the violence of the masses; they must also combine the masses' political forces with the people's armed forces and the armed struggle with the masses' political struggle, thus turning them into uprisings and war of all the people.

Only by correctly and thoroughly understanding this way of looking at violence can we organize and mobilize the forces of all our people and of the entire country to fight the aggressors. Not only do we have an army with which to fight the aggressors, but our people also fight them with every appropriate means. Our people not only step up production and support combat but also directly engage in fighting the aggressors.

We not only conduct an armed struggle but also have the benefit of the masses' fierce political struggle. We also attack the aggressors by recruiting troops and gaining enemy converts.

We not only conduct military attacks but also enjoy the masses' uprisings on every scale and in various forms. We make use of the uprisings of all the people and the people's

war to fight the aggressors. Our people's present fight against
the aggressors bears new characteristics, namely, a high sense
of national enlightenment and class enlightenment among the
masses, a very scientific, tight, and widespread organization,
and very flexible methods of carrying on the struggle.

All of this has, therefore, caused all our people—the 31
million Vietnamese people—to become valiant combatants in
killing the aggressors for national salvation. The lines "the
entire country animated by the same mind and all the people
fight the aggressors" have been reflected in these ways: organizing and mobilizing all the people to fight the aggressors; building the people's political and armed forces; using
the people's armed forces, with the three troop categories as
the core forces to fight the aggressors; relying on the masses'
political forces; building everywhere the bases and rear base
areas of the people's war from "have not" to "have," from
small to big, and from imperfect to perfect; combining the
local rear base area with the country-wide rear base area,
while relying on the internal rear base area, namely the
socialist camp; creatively applying the method of waging war
and the military art of the revolutionary war; fighting larger
enemy forces with our own smaller forces; using weak forces
to fight strong forces; attacking the aggressors with the combined strength of the armed and political struggles on various
strategic operational theaters, in both the rural areas and the
cities; defeating the aggressors step by step, and advancing
toward defeating them completely; strengthening the Party's
leadership over the war, and considering this a main factor
in deciding success.

In general, our experiences are essentially those of armed
uprisings, revolutionary war, and national liberation war to
regain power and to overthrow the imperialists' yokes, and
they are also partially those of a war to defend the fatherland,
as our administration is prepared to fight foreign aggressors.
We should strive to study further and to develop our experiences, not only to serve the immediate struggle to defeat the

U.S. aggressors completely but also to defend the fatherland for a long time to come.

Our Party's military line originated from our Party's correct political line, from the Marxist theory of war and armed forces, from the intelligence and strategic abilities of our ancestors, and from the experiences of the world's advanced revolutionary struggles. It profoundly reflects the realities of our people's multiform revolutionary struggle for the past forty years under our Party's leadership. This military line, since its formation and during its development, has proved itself to be always correct and to have an invincible strength, because it originates directly from and is always guided by our Party's correct political line and always relies on the masses' tremendous strength and inexhaustible force of initiatives.

The strength of the revolutionary war is the centralized manifestation of the all-out strength of the revolution, from the correct revolutionary task to the correct political objective of people's war, from the scientific disposition of the great revolutionary force to the line of building a powerful force of the people's war, and from the correct view of revolutionary violence to that of the uprising and war of all the people.

This is the very close dialectical relationship between the military and political lines and the strength of our people's revolutionary war. In the situation of a continuous war, our Party's military line has always been thoroughly examined through the realities of the war, has been constantly improved and developed, and has scored repeated successes in theory as well as in practice. It is the invincible weapon with which our people will defeat all imperialist aggressors and their rotten and reactionary military science and theories.

PART 3. *The Mobilization and Organization of the Entire People to Fight the Aggressors, and the Building of the Powerful Political and Armed Forces of the Revolutionary War and Uprising.*

To conduct a people's war, it is necessary to adopt a correct line in building up forces. This is the line of mobilizing, arming, and motivating the entire people to participate in all types of uprising and war, and in building up a widespread mass political force—with the three categories of people's armed forces as nucleus forces—to stage a nationwide struggle against aggression. This line is a creative application of Marxist-Leninist thoughts on mobilizing and arming the entire people and building a new type of revolutionary army according to a realistic appraisal of conditions in our country. It shows an understanding of the concept that revolutionary violence is the masses' violence in building up the forces of revolutionary war. It inherits and develops to a new level the tradition of nationwide anti-invasion struggle, in which everyone must be a soldier and every woman must fight the enemy when he invades her home. This is a long-standing tradition in the history of our people's heroic wars for national liberation and defense.

To conduct a people's war, it is necessary to mobilize the entire people. This is a fundamental concept in our Party's line of building people's war forces. Lenin said: "To conduct war, it is necessary to mobilize all people's forces, to turn the entire country into a revolutionary bastion, to devote everything to the war, and to use all forces and national resources to protect the revolution." To mobilize and organize the entire population to participate in the uprising and war is our Party's method of educating and organizing the masses widely, deeply, and constantly, from the lower to the upper levels and in accordance with a correct revolutionary line.

Since our Party's birth, the method of its revolutionary

26

campaign has been to direct propaganda, to organize and lead the masses to struggle, from the lower to the upper levels, and to motivate them to rise up and regain administrative power through revolutionary violence. Because of the widespread mobilization and organization of the masses to fight vigorously in the 1930–31 revolutionary movement, in the 1936–39 democratic campaign period, and in the 1940–45 national liberation campaign period, the great forces of the entire people were able to rise up to fight aggression during the August Revolution as well as during the anti-French resistance and the present anti-U.S. resistance.

In partial uprisings, our Party, which consisted of secret political and armed organs, motivated its bases in each locality to arise valiantly to overthrow the enemy's local administration and establish the revolutionary administration, to promote local guerrilla warfare, to step up political and armed struggles, to develop speedily the masses' and revolutionary armed forces; and to boost vigorously country-wide revolutionary fervor in preparation for the general thrust to wrest political power by force.

In the general uprising, the Party motivated all northern and southern people to adhere to the broad national united front and to arise simultaneously throughout cities and rural areas in order to smash the imperialists' and feudalists' yokes and to regain power for the people.

After the revolutionary war, [because the country] possessed an improved and stable rear base area as well as an administration of the people, the mobilization and organization of the masses for combat were on a much larger and more comprehensive scale. Under the slogans "Entire People's Resistance," "Comprehensive Resistance," and "Everything for Victory," all the people's forces were mobilized to the maximum, to serve the task of defeating the aggressors.

Even during the war, our Party emphasized propaganda to motivate the organization and improvement of people's forces, unremittingly broadened the people's political force, and developed the people's armed forces, with the purpose of mobilizing the entire population to fight. To motivate all the people to take part in the uprisings and war, it was necessary to build mass political force as well as to build up the people's army.

Our political force is a force of all the people that participates in uprisings and wars in an organized manner under the Party's vanguard leadership. It includes revolutionary classes, patriotic elements, and nationalities in our country who have assembled in a broad, united national front, under working class leadership, with the worker-peasant alliance as a foundation.

Our political force is a firm, steady foundation on which to build and develop comprehensive forces for the revolutionary war, to protect the material and moral forces on the political, military, economic, and cultural fronts, on the front line and in the rear base areas and to form and develop the people's armed revolutionary forces.

The people's armed forces cannot exist or grow strong without the revolutionaries or the people's strong political force, whose core is the worker-peasant class organized and led by the Party. The people's armed forces have developed from weak to strong forces during the period of implementing the systems of voluntary and compulsory military service, from the first worker-peasant self-defense units in the Nghe-Tinh Soviet movement in 1930–31 to the national salvation troops, the Vietnam propaganda units of the Liberation Army, the Ba To guerrillas, and thousands of self-defense and combat self-defense units in all localities in the pre-August Revolution period. They have come from enlightened and organized revolutionaries.

Relying on these firm, numerous political forces, our armed forces, under Party leadership, have displayed a fine revolutionary spirit. In the face of great opportunities and turning points in the war, we have steadfastly and rapidly developed and strengthened our people's armed forces. Realities emerging from the revolutionary struggle in our country clearly show that the mass political forces also constitute an offensive force that attack the enemy with revolutionary violence in both uprisings and revolutionary war, but especially in uprisings. The coordination of our political forces with our people's armed forces has been extremely inspiring.

Further developing the experience acquired in the August Revolution and, under new historical conditions, in the anti-French resistance, the southern masses' political forces under the banner of the National Liberation Front of South Vietnam have developed their extremely great strength in the protracted, resolute struggle against every attempt at domination and every form of the neo-colonialist, aggressive war by the U.S. imperialists. It is reasonable to say that the southern people's political forces are more powerful than ever. They have played the main, decisive role in the victory of the great spontaneous uprising. In coordination with the people's armed forces, they have defeated the special war strategy and are defeating the limited war strategy of the U.S. imperialists.

The presence of an army concerned with political struggle in the war has been a striking initiative in the organization of forces for the present South Vietnam revolutionary war. The army for political struggle was organized and based on the masses' strong political force and on workers and farmers. It includes excellent and valiant elements of the masses, of all social strata and of all ages. There are agents in the plains, mountains, rural areas, and cities. It is carefully organized and militarized, thus fighting in a revolutionary and scientific manner by using extremely varied and lively means of combat. It is the core force of the masses' political struggle in the present South Vietnam revolution and revolutionary war.

Armed uprisings and revolutionary wars are the highest forms of struggle in the revolution to wrest and maintain power. No uprisings or wars lack armed forces. Therefore, to prepare for and to carry on our armed uprisings and revolutionary war, as well as to build a political force, our Party particularly emphasized the building of the people's armed forces as a basis for the struggle of all our people against aggressors. Under the Party's glorious banner, our people's armed forces were born and raised in the entire population's fierce, revolutionary struggle based on the people's political force.

Our army is truly a people's army, born of the people and fighting for them. In twenty years, it has gradually developed from guerrilla units and masses' self-defense units into independent armed groups; from small guerrilla cells into increasingly concentrated units, including main-force, regional, and militia units; and from poorly equipped infantry units into armed forces with numerous branches and services operating with modern equipment. Our Party's line and stand toward building up the people's armed forces have increasingly improved in this direction.

The problem of the army's class nature and revolutionary substance is the key one in our Party's theory of building up armed forces. As asserted by our Party, our armed forces belong to the people—especially laborers, workers, and peasants—and are led by the Party of the working class. They include, above all and in essence, outstanding elements of the revolutionary class, of the worker-peasant alliance, and of the people of various nationalities on Vietnamese territory. They are a tool used by the Party and the revolutionary state to conduct the revolutionary struggle and armed struggle to carry out the Party's revolutionary tasks. As the armed forces of the people's democratic state, they previously assumed the functions of worker-peasant dictatorship, and they are now carrying out the historic tasks of proletarian dictatorship. Their duty is to protect the [victory of the] revolution and the people's administration and to resist every internal and external enemy.

It is a fighting army as well as a working and producing one. It is of working-class nature. Its stand and thoughts are those of the working class and of Marxism-Leninism. At the time when our armed forces were mere guerrilla units, as well as when they became stronger, with branches and services using modern equipment, our Party constantly emphasized the strengthening of the army's class nature, considering it the best guarantee and basic factor in creating the armed forces' fighting strength.

This becomes more important in a country in which the majority of the people are peasants and bourgeois and the leading class—the working class—is not numerous. In the first days of building up the Red worker-and-peasant army, Lenin considered strengthening the working element one of the most important measures in strengthening the revolutionary nature of the Soviet armed forces. In our country, starting from the existing conditions of our Vietnamese society and armed forces, our Party considered as essential measures to reinforce the armed forces' revolutionary nature: strengthening its leadership vis-à-vis the armed forces; teaching proletarian thoughts; and building up the armed forces' political stand, along with strengthening the working-and-farming element, especially among the armed forces' cadres.

The essential problems in building our armed forces in the political field during our army's development have been the unremitting consolidation and strengthening of the Party's absolute, direct, and comprehensive leadership vis-à-vis the people's armed forces—the most fundamental principle; the unremitting strengthening of the political task—the source of strength and a principle of building the people's armed forces; the extreme emphasis on the task of political teaching and thought-leading in the army, so that all cadres and soldiers will be keenly aware of the Party's political line and task, military line and task, and stands, policies, and state laws; instruction in Marxism-Leninism, the increased development of class awareness, coordinated with national awareness, education in patriotism, love of socialism, and the international proletarian spirit, and, on this basis, the unremitting effort to heighten the armed forces' combativeness and determination to fight and to win; the continuing consolidation of the Party's organization and the organization of political tasks; the active formation and training of an army of cadres absolutely faithful to the Party's revolutionary enterprise and expert in leading, organizing, and commanding; the implementation of a centralized democratic regime and a severe, just, and self-conscious discipline, that of a revolutionary army, on the basis of broadening internal democracy; the firm strengthening of internal solidarity—the solidarity between army and people that must be similar to the one between fish and water, and close international solidarity.

In this way, our people's armed forces developed a satisfactory revolutionary character, being loyal to the Party and faithful to the people, fighting without fear, sacrificing themselves for the independence and freedom of the fatherland and for socialism, and considering themselves the tool of the workers' and peasants' dictatorship during the phase of the people's national and democratic revolution. They have moved toward successfully carrying out their task of being the tool of the proletarian dictatorship during the phase of the socialist revolution.

On the basis of building the armed forces politically, our Party must successfully settle the problem of building them organizationally. In our country, experience in implementing people's war over the past twenty-five years has proved that the three categories of troops—main-force units, regional forces, and guerrilla and self-defense militia forces—are the most appropriate organizational way in which to mobilize all of the population to fight the enemy.

Great attention must be paid to building up main-force units as well as regional forces. The building up of main-force units must be closely associated with the building up of regional forces, on-the-spot forces, and mobile forces. In forming our army, we have developed our forefathers' traditions of organizing a force of all the people for the war.

Self-defense militia forces are the broad armed forces of the laboring people who are still engaged in production. They act as an instrument of violence used by the public administrations at the lower levels. In hamlets, villages, industrial enterprises, and city wards, they are organized according to combat tasks, conditions, and characteristics. They form a steady, strong force, widespread throughout the country, ready to fight and fight well with all kinds of weapons, from rudimentary to modern ones, and with highly efficient combat methods.

They have satisfactorily carried out the tasks of directly protecting the people, firmly maintaining and developing political bases, engaging in production, and supplying regional forces and main-force units with good cadres and combatants.

Regional forces are core forces of the armed struggle in local situations. They are activated according to the tasks and practical conditions of each battlefield and locality to become strong units of high quality—with the necessary armed branches capable of concentrated fighting in localities in close coordination with self-defense militia and main-force units—and are capable of outstanding fulfillment of such tasks as annihilating the enemy, initiating a guerrilla war, protecting the local population and administrations and firmly maintaining the local people's rule.

Main-force units are mobile armed forces in charge of nationwide battlefields or a number of definite strategic operational areas. They have the necessary armed branches and services, namely, very strong infantry units, and also consistently proportional air and naval forces. Main-force units must be of high combat quality. They must be strong enough to fight important annihilating battles and deal the enemy increasingly heavy blows. They must be invincible and must swiftly and neatly annihilate increasingly large enemy units in order to change the battle situation in our favor.

Therefore, the people's armed forces must satisfactorily carry out not only their main duty of annihilating the enemy but also the tasks of protecting the people and contributing toward and participating in the building and development of the masses' political forces, which serve as a core of a war of all the people against the enemy.

In view of the characteristics of the revolutionary war in

our country and of the increasingly fierce war conditions, especially when the enemy has implemented a neo-colonialist aggressive policy, we must form main-force units of increasingly high combat quality and take interest in activating really strong regional armed forces. Only then will the three categories of troops be able to develop to the utmost their combat strength, to achieve close coordination in annihilating the enemy, to protect effectively the people's comprehensive forces, to maintain our rule firmly, to develop people's war strongly and comprehensively, and to win ever greater victories.

Closely combined with the political force and the public-security armed force, the three troop categories have been organized and built according to a suitable and proportionate scope and rationally deployed in each strategic theater, battlefield, and locality, to insure that both local and mobile forces are strong and to combine closely and specifically local forces with mobile forces at lower and national levels.

This is a typical feature of the problem of building forces in a people's war and, at the same time, an outstanding advantage of people's war in our country. Having a strong knowledge of local geography, [we must] keep a firm hold on the enemy situation, hitting him accurately and, furthermore, attacking him as soon as he arrives in any given place. We must erode, annihilate, disperse, and [harass] the enemy everywhere, creating conditions for mobile forces to launch concentrated blows to annihilate him wherever his gaps are exposed.

Because our territory is narrow, our people's war widespread, and because the enemy has a high mobility and a large troop strength, by using such an organization and deployment, we can restrict his strength and develop our own, creating the steady strategic deployment position of people's war needed to maintain our initiative in attacking the enemy under any circumstances. This insures that we always have enough forces to attack the enemy everywhere, while being able to mass a strong regular force capable of defeating his strategic mobile army and successfully winning greater and greater victories in the war without needing to have a permanent troop strength superior or equal to his.

Along with the development of the revolution and the maturation of the armed forces, our army has proceeded from the voluntary military service system to the compulsory military service system, a new step to advance the mobilization of the entire population for participation in building up the people's armed forces and strengthening the national defense. Initially, our army was merely composed of small guerrilla groups, born in the process of the people's revolutionary struggle, who arose to resist with bare hands imperialism and its lackeys.

We then advocated relying on the people to build the army through the voluntary military service system that we applied throughout the anti-French resistance war. After peace was restored, the completely liberated north advanced toward building socialism with a perfected state and every institution of an independent nation.

Faced with the requirements of the revolutionary task in our country—which call for strengthening the national defense of all the people with a permanent, [words indistinct] crack army coupled with a really strong reserve force, combining economy with national defense, advancing, as a new step, the armament of the entire people and the [popularization?] of the entire army, fully developing the people's right to rule, realizing an equitable contribution among the entire population to the task of defending the fatherland and, at the same time, aiming at overcoming the weakness due to the long application of the entirely voluntary military service system—the Party advocated advancing toward a compulsory military service system.

This is a new development and a new success in the task of building the people's army, arming and [popularizing?] the entire people, and consolidating our people's national defense. Along with realizing the compulsory military service system, we must step up general military training, step up the national defense physical-training and sports movement, build a military style of living, and disseminate military knowledge widely among the entire people, especially among youth, in order to prepare them practically to do their military duty and to defend the fatherland.

Arms and equipment are the material and technical base of combat armies, the basic element of their strength. To increase an army's fighting power, it is necessary to improve its equipment constantly.

Applying the Marxist-Leninist view of the relationship between men and weapons—that if men are the factors deciding victories in war, weapons and equipment are very important and essential—and acting according to our country's actual circumstances and the reality of our revolutionary war, our Party has settled the problem of our armed forces' weapons and equipment.

Our Party has correctly decided that the masses are the source of our armed forces' equipment. Our armed forces must arm themselves with any available equipment, produce it themselves, take weapons from the enemy to kill him, and, to improve their supplies of equipment constantly, obtain aid from fraternal socialist countries when conditions permit.

During the first phase of forming our armed forces, because our economy was backward, because we lacked weapon-manufacturing bases, and because our country was completely encircled by the imperialists, our armed forces encountered many difficulties in equipping themselves. Relying on the masses and applying the motto "fight with any available weapon," our Party mobilized the population to do their utmost to provide our armed forces with any necessary equipment to fight the enemy. Thus, the Party surmounted all difficulties in producing part of the needed weapons and ammunition.

Moreover, our Party, with foresight, urged our armed forces to find a source of equipment on the front line, to take weapons from the enemy with which to arm themselves, and to use these enemy weapons to shoot at his head. During the anti-French resistance, our armed forces were mainly equipped with modern weapons taken from the enemy. We received aid from fraternal socialist countries only later, as of 1950.

Since the restoration of peace, we have relied on our ever growing socialist economy and on the great assistance from the fraternal socialist countries to modernize and improve our armed forces' equipment on a large scale. Thus, during the anti-U.S., national salvation struggle, despite our under-developed national defense industry, we have quickly achieved great leaps forward in qualitatively improving our armed forces' equipment.

Besides doing this for our infantry, we have quickly developed other modern military services—such as the anti-aircraft force and the air force—to defeat U.S. aggression.

Relying on the above-mentioned sources of equipment, taking into account the actual situation of our country, the line of all people fighting the enemy, and the military objectives and military art of people's war, and to develop our strong point—the fact that we are fighting the enemy in our own country—our Party advocates the necessity of associating modern and relatively modern weapons with rudimentary weapons, and of continually improving and modernizing our weapons and equipment in such a way that the fighting power of our three forces and all our people will increase.

Our regular and regional troops have been equipped mainly with modern and relatively modern weapons and equipment. But rudimentary ones must be used exhaustively in training and combat. Our self-defense militiamen have paid great attention to developing rudimentary weapons. Simultaneously, they have gradually, appropriately, and partially equipped themselves, especially in their core units, with modern and relatively modern weapons.

The realities of war in our country have demonstrated that if modern weapons play an important role in the annihilation of the enemy, rudimentary weapons are very efficient in helping all the population to participate in this annihilation. Along with improving the quality of weapons and equipment, we

have endeavored to heighten the level of production and man-
agement of various categories of weapons and to improve the
capacity to handle these weapons, in accordance with the
military line and ideology of our Party and actual conditions
on the battlefields in our country.

The building and training of a cadre organization is a very
important problem, a key point in the task of building up the
armed forces. Our armed forces, developed from nothing, have
a large cadre organization that is absolutely faithful to the
revolutionary enterprise of the Party and people. They have
been and are constantly being trained and seasoned in the
revolutionary struggle and the long, hard armed struggle,
and they have successfully completed the tasks entrusted to
them by the Party and people. Based on the masses' strength,
the cadre organization built and improved by the Party has
met, quantitatively and qualitatively, the requirements of the
regular and reserve forces, in peace and war, and has served,
in time, all the complicated building and combat tasks of the
armed forces in the war. This is the great achievement of our
Party's activity concerning cadres.

In building the cadre organization, our Party set forth a
correct line for the task concerning cadres and set and improved the class trend and the norms and policy toward army
cadres. Our Party has always firmly held to the class line, considering the working class the main one. Our Party attaches
importance to the selection, improvement, and promotion of
outstanding cadres taken from the worker-peasant class; at
the same time, it selects, improves, and promotes cadres from
among outstanding intellectuals who have close relations with
workers and peasants and who have wholeheartedly served
the revolution. In carrying out our Party's policy and task
concerning cadres, we have fought all tendencies to devi-
ate from class policy, have fought neglect in the task of improving outstanding persons from the worker-peasant class,
and have fought narrow-minded sectarianism.

Our Party has constantly trained and improved our armed
forces cadres to make them more virtuous and talented, to

consolidate their class standpoint, and to strengthen their intense patriotism and their readiness to fight and sacrifice their lives for the independence and freedom of our fatherland and for socialism. It has trained the cadres to strengthen their absolute loyalty to the revolution, to keep a firm and constant hold on and resolutely to implement the Party's political and military line, to establish close relations with the masses, to heighten their technical and specialist level, to understand fully modern military theories, and to improve their ability to organize cleverly the execution of all tasks under difficult and complex conditions.

In each phase, our Party has actively applied appropriate measures to improve cadres. It has continually paid special attention to training cadres according to the realities of the revolutionary struggle of the masses, especially combat realities, aiming at constant training to improve the body of cadres both qualitatively and quantitatively.

With regard to building up our people's armed forces, we have satisfactorily solved the problems on quality and quantity, paying attention to both but regarding quality as more important. The view that quality is more important is a key feature of our people's military tradition. "Crack troops are not needed in large numbers"—this was the view of Tran Huong Dao and Nguyen Hue, national heroes who used their well-trained armies to defeat the aggressors' much larger armies. The quality of armed forces is the result of a combination of men and weapons and of various factors—military, political, logistical, ideological, organizational, technical, and fighting methods—with human, political, and moral factors being the most decisive ones.

Army-building and combat realities have clearly shown that a high-quality army is one that possesses a high combat morale, an intense determination to attack the enemy, satisfactory technical and tactical levels, skillful fighting methods, neat, light, and scattered organizational patterns, good equipment, and a cadre corps and command units that have firm organizational capabilities, discipline, a stanch perseverance, and high mobility in all terrains and under all weather conditions, and whose material and technical requirements are adequately and satisfactorily met.

In qualitative improvement, the three troop categories have different requirements. The self-defense militia organization must be very widespread, firm, and strong. The regional forces and main-force units must be highly seasoned and must have adequate strength.

Our population is not very large. Our army is usually smaller than the aggressor army. Therefore, our army's quality must be demonstrated by its great strategic effectiveness and high combat efficiency. Strategically, we usually employ a smaller army to fight and defeat a larger and better-equipped enemy army. In campaigns and in combat, we use forces with smaller strength and fewer weapons than the enemy to annihilate him and win great victories.

If all of our units are of a high quality and are capable of fighting the enemy with high combat efficiency, we can greatly increase the combat strength of our limited armed forces and, at the same time, reduce organizational and leadership problems, replenish our forces, meet our army's material requirements, and use our forces economically. This represents a major problem of strategic importance.

To insure that the more our armed forces fight, the greater vitality they acquire and the greater victories they win in a protracted, resolute struggle, we have implemented the motto "fighting while building and developing our forces." We fight in order to build and develop our forces. We build and develop our forces in order to fight vigorously and win greater victories. We have coordinated the gradual with the rapid development of our forces, in order to seize every opportunity to advance the war toward victory.

Our Party's line in regard to building up our armed forces was formulated and has been developed more and more perfectly in our people's protracted revolutionary and armed struggles. In implementing this line, our armed forces have developed and matured rapidly and resolutely, acquiring an invincible combat strength and winning glorious victories.

This represents the essence of our Party's viewpoint on building forces in the people's war. Realities emerging from the revolutionary war in our country have proved that this viewpoint is completely correct. Its enormous strength has been demonstrated by the fact that, by basing ourselves upon this correct viewpoint, we have mobilized, trained, and organized the strength of all our armed forces and people into a firm block, a steel-like body that has insured a highly scientific distribution of combat tasks, and that has formed a great combat force for attacking the enemy continuously and defeating every aggressor army, no matter how cruel and how large it may be and no matter what modern equipment it may possess.

This viewpoint was demonstrated most substantially and lucidly in President Ho's great appeal in which he said: "Our 31 million compatriots in both parts of the country, regardless of age and sex, must be 31 million courageous American-annihilating, national salvation combatants who are determined to win final victory." *

* President Ho's talk at a solemn meeting held in 1967 to commemorate the anniversaries of the founding of the Vietnamese People's Army and of the National Resistance Day.—HANOI RADIO

PART 4. *To Wage a War Properly, It Is Necessary to Possess a Firmly Organized Rear Base Area.* * The Rear Base Area Is Always Necessary for Success Because It is a Source of Supply for Human and Material Resources for the War and a Source of Political and Spiritual Motivation and Encouragement for the Front Line. Without a Stable Rear Base Area, the Front Line Cannot Defeat the Aggressors. This Is the General Law for Every War.*

The problem that our Party faced was how could our people—barehanded, without an inch of free land as a base, with only a small country and population, and with a backward agricultural economy—struggle to liberate themselves and to build firm bases and rear areas for the people's war to defeat the imperialist aggressors.

Our Party creatively resolved this problem and, in the process of its long revolutionary struggle, accumulated many valuable experiences in how to build political bases, and bases and rear areas, for the uprising of all the people and the people's war and the revolutionary war under the actual conditions and circumstances in our country.

First: It learned to rely completely on the people and to proceed from building the masses' political bases to building bases and rear areas, from "have not" to "have," from small to big, and from imperfect to ever more perfect:

In our national history, each time our people fought to gain or protect their national independence our forefathers and fathers knew how to build their bases. They paid attention to the friendliness of the people and the favorable features of the terrain. Sometimes they established their bases in forests, mountains, and, occasionally, in the swampy plains. At other times they favored the deltas, gathering capable men and material resources among the people to build and develop their forces.

* Nikolai Lenin, *Collected Works,* XXVII, 54–55.—GIAP

42

After the emergence of our Party and after it set out on the path of revolution through violence—the path of armed uprising and revolutionary war—that was designed to seize the administration and to topple the enemy of the class and the people, the problem of building bases was also posed.

In line with the development of the revolutionary struggle, we have proceeded from building political bases toward building bases and rear base areas and creating increasingly larger rear base areas, from "have not" to "have," from small to big, and from fragmented to systematized. We now have a perfect national defense foundation of all the people in the socialist north. It can be said that, at the outset, when our Party set forth the policy of preparing for the armed struggle and uprising, we did not have a single inch of free land.

At that time, our sole prop was the revolutionary organization of the people and their already enlightened patriotism and boundless loyalty toward the revolutionary undertaking. Relying on this patriotism, our Party did its best to conduct a revolutionary drive to educate, mobilize, and lead the masses in the various forms of their political struggle and in this way to develop its own and the masses' political organizations, to build political bases everywhere, and to see to it that wherever the masses were, there would be a political base and a revolutionary organization.

From those political bases, using the motto that "armed political propaganda is more important than military matters" —which President Ho set forth for the first guerrilla units— our Party did its best to build secret armed bases and, from bottom to top, to step up political struggle in combination with armed struggle.

Following this, our Party advanced toward guerrilla warfare and the phased armed uprising and building of the Viet Bac Liberation Zone, as well as a number of guerrilla bases in other localities, all the while vigorously and broadly developing political bases throughout the country, increasing the masses' revolutionary fervor, and advancing toward successfully conducting the general uprising, seizing the administration on a nationwide basis, and founding the Democratic Republic of Vietnam.

During the long resistance against the French imperialist aggressors, we did our best to defend and consolidate our vast free areas—using them as the firm rear base areas for the people's war—while fighting continually to enlarge the guerrilla-infested areas and guerrilla bases that had been established throughout the enemy rear area.

The increasingly and comprehensively consolidated rear base area of the resistance was a source of great political and moral encouragement, a source of supplies to satisfy the growing needs of the front line. In areas under the enemy's temporary control, the building of bases essentially followed this pattern: Through various forms of struggle—from illegal to legal struggle, from economic to political and armed struggle—and through the fierce fight against the enemy, the clandestine political bases of the masses gradually turned the areas under the enemy's temporary control into guerrilla-infested areas and guerrilla bases that, small and isolated at first, became linked together into increasingly vast areas.

Nowadays, the southerners—who rose up to liberate themselves—have a large and solid rear base area, which is the socialist north. They are also endeavoring to build their own bases and rear base area in the liberated sectors.

These expanding liberated areas have been having an increasingly great and diversified impact on the southern revolutionary war. Creatively applying past experiences on how to build the bases and rear base area to [conform with] new historical conditions, the southerners have not only built solid bases in the mountainous areas and deltas, which are crisscrossed by rivers and canals, but have also succeeded in building solid footholds, even in strategic areas near a number of cities where the enemy has set up military posts.

The liberated areas—where enemy posts are still present—have appeared close to the enemy's large bases. These are the areas where the U.S. puppets still have their military posts, sometimes in relatively large numbers. Although the enemy has resorted to many cruel military or crafty political tricks, he has been unable to set up his oppressive machinery.

On the other hand, by their resolute, courageous, and creative struggle, the southern people have succeeded in maintaining their power there, seriously encircling and threatening the enemy's bases and rear.

After the victorious resistance against the French colonialists, the north entered the socialist revolutionary phase. It has become an independent and socialist state with a complete national administrative structure. It has endeavored to reinforce its forces in all fields and to consolidate the national defense system of all the people. It has become the stable and powerful revolutionary base for the entire country. During the anti-U.S., national salvation struggle, the north has become the great rear for the great southern front line. It has developed its great [efforts?] on the anti-U.S., national salvation undertaking of our people.

Second: Our Party learned to rely on the revolutionary strength in both rural and urban areas, to build solid bases and rears in rural areas while building revolutionary bases in cities, and to associate the local rear base areas everywhere with the common rear base of the entire country.

Our revolutionary war depends on the entire people's strength and on regular forces comprised of workers and peasants fighting the enemy here on our territory and using all means to coordinate attacks in rural and urban areas. For this reason, we can and must rely on our revolutionary strength in these areas, and we must build firm bases in the countryside and revolutionary structures in the cities. In rural areas embracing the jungles, mountains, and plains, we have a revolutionary force, including the bulk of peasants and laborers, or 90 per cent of our total population, equipped with revolutionary determination, a self-sufficient and self-supplying local economy independent from the cities and very suitable for launching and maintaining our people's war against the aggressive war, despite the enemy's material and technical predominance, and a terrain favorable for our people's armed forces' struggle. The enemy's ruling machinery, however, has proved to be relatively weak and has revealed many deficiencies.

The countryside, jungles, and mountains, with their dangerous terrains, are important military strategic areas where the ethnic peoples are very eager for and loyal to the revolution. [In these areas] the enemy reveals almost all of his weaknesses and gaps. Relying on these very solid bases of the revolution and revolutionary war, our people can maintain, build, and develop their forces, and can persist in a protracted struggle under the most difficult circumstances. These bases can serve as starting points from which we can expand our struggle to the plains.

The rural and delta areas are densely populated areas with enormous resources, which the aggressor enemy has constantly tried to occupy, in the hope of scraping together human and material resources and thereby implementing his policy of using Vietnamese to fight Vietnamese and war to support war.

If we succeed in gaining control over the rural areas, the revolution will acquire a firm basis for mobilizing human and material resources to develop its forces for protracted combat, to insure that the more the revolutionary forces fight, the more powerful they become—thus bankrupting the enemy's policy of trying to obtain human and material resources and using Vietnamese to fight Vietnamese and war to support war —and to create favorable conditions for the rural, delta, and mountainous areas, so that the urban revolutionary movement can be supported vigorously and the enemy attacked at his nerve centers and in his lair.

Obviously, the rural areas constitute the stable, long-term base and battleground of the revolutionary war in our country. Firmly relying on the rural areas and building solid strongholds in the rural, mountainous, and delta areas are strategic requirements of the revolutionary war in our country. While building strong, stable bases in the rural areas, our Party has attached great importance to building revolutionary bases in the urban areas.

The urban areas are the places where the working class is concentrated. The working class possesses the highest revolutionary spirit and is both the leading class and the force that, together with the peasants and laborers, forms the main-force army of the revolution. The forces that have a fairly high patriotic, anti-imperialist spirit—numerous strata of laborers, students, and progressive intellectuals—are also concentrated in the urban areas.

The urban areas, especially the major cities and townships, are the enemy's political, military, economic, and cultural centers, where his leading support and his principal repressive facilities are concentrated. The urban areas represent the enemy's strong points compared with the rural areas. But the enemy also has political and military weaknesses in urban areas, especially in the political field. His basic scheme is strenuously to transform the urban areas into the safe rear base of the aggressive war.

To advance the revolutionary war toward victory, we must build revolutionary bases in the urban areas and create conditions for attacking the enemy directly in the cities in every suitable way, thereby, depriving him of a safe rear base. We must also insure close coordination between the urban revolutionary forces and the rural revolutionary forces in order to attack the enemy directly in his lair, insure that the revolutionary war annihilates more and more extensively his military and political forces, extend the people's control from lower to higher echelons and from small to large areas, and advance toward winning final victory.

The coordination between building firm strongholds in the rural areas and building revolutionary bases in the urban areas contributed to creating the unique feature of uprisings in the Vietnamese revolution—as demonstrated by the August Revolution—and to executing successfully the strategy of fighting on a protracted basis, and, at the same time, to stimulating the urban struggle movement during the anti-French resistance.

This coordination has made and is making an important

contribution to great victories in the three strategic areas of the southern revolutionary war. In compliance with the rule governing the development of the revolutionary war's rear base, and to exploit, mobilize, and fully develop the total forces of our country, we have advocated combining the building of local rear bases everywhere, along with the common rear base of our entire country. Our experience has clearly shown that we must not only build common strongholds and rear bases for the entire country but also build strongholds and rear bases everywhere, on every battlefield and in each locality.

The tasks involved in building these strongholds and rear bases in every locality, battlefield, and echelon, from the basic echelon upward, are closely associated with our Party's line on mobilizing all the people and the entire country to fight the aggressors and with the policy of building firm, strong local forces everywhere for the people's war. This conforms with the conditions of our country, which is not very large, and with the methods of waging the people's war, in which our people have been determined to stand firm, to attack the enemy everywhere, and not to budge even one inch.

In implementing this line and this policy, we have used fully and developed successfully the strength and rule of our people and of the new social system that has taken shape and that is being consolidated in the liberated areas promptly to meet urgent and local combat requirements.

In our present anti-U.S., national salvation struggle, we have coordinated local strongholds and rear bases in the south with the entire country's huge rear base, the socialist north, which is linked with the vast socialist camp.

This coordination insures the development of the strength of all our people, of the socialist regime in the north and the new social regime in the liberated area of South Vietnam, and the development of the strength of the entire revolutionary achievement of our people in the past scores of years of continuous struggle to defeat the imperialists' ringleaders. Basically, this clearly shows that in the present resistance war, our people are strong enough and are able to stand steadfastly, as in the previous resistance against the French.

Third: Our Party learned to develop strongly the active offensive spirit, to endeavor to develop comprehensively the strongholds and real bases, to struggle positively to defend our rear base area and, at the same time, actively attack enemy rear areas, turn them into our front lines, and constantly expand our strongholds and rear bases.

As far as the revolutionary war is concerned, in the process of building our strongholds and rear bases by starting from nothing, the creation of the first strongholds is only an initial success. To strengthen and develop this success, to help strongholds and rear bases stand fast against all challenges and to develop ever more strongly their impact toward the war, it is absolutely necessary to strengthen constantly and comprehensively our strongholds and rear bases.

According to the viewpoint of people's war, the strengthening of the strongholds and rear bases primarily depends on political, economic, military, and geographical factors, of which the most important are the political and human factors and the nature of the social regime. Therefore, the building of the rear bases must be comprehensive and must include the various political, economic, military, and cultural aspects.

It is first necessary to build a sound political position, to strengthen the political and moral consensus among the people; to strive constantly to develop the supremacy of the new social regime in various aspects—political, economic, and cultural; to achieve democratic reforms gradually and actively; to improve the material and spiritual life of the people; and to develop constantly the latent potentials of the rear bases, with which they will be able to defend themselves and, at the same time, develop comprehensively their great contributions toward the war. The strongholds and rear bases of people's war pose a constant threat to the enemy, and thus are the objectives of the enemy's repeated and violent attacks.

Therefore, the question of strengthening the strongholds and rear bases must be closely connected with the struggle for the defense of the rear bases and the expansion and development of the comprehensive contributions of the strongholds and rear bases. It is necessary to develop strongly the active offensive spirit and to coordinate closely the active struggle to defend our rear bases with the active attacks against the enemy rear areas, thus transforming the enemy rear areas into our battlefields.

Attacks—strong attacks—are the best way to defend and broaden our rear bases, to shrink the enemy rear areas, and to develop strongly and comprehensively the contribution of our rear bases. This is also the essential requirement of the building of the strongholds and rear bases of the liberation war, starting from nothing—from small to large scale—and aiming at regaining, maintaining, and developing—from partially to comprehensively—the people's right to rule.

In the resistance against the French, the basic aim in defending our freedom was to step up attacks against the enemy rear areas and to develop guerrilla warfare. This was closely coordinated with the constant, comprehensive strengthening of our rear bases and the active struggle for the defense of the free zones against all enemy attacks. Because of this policy, our free zones could be secured and strengthened, guerrilla bases and areas could be constantly built in enemy rear areas, and our rear bases could be constantly expanded while the enemy rear areas increasingly shrank.

The southern armed forces and people in the southern revolutionary war creatively applied and developed these experiences. With a fierce offensive spirit in actively consolidating the liberated areas in every respect, and in positively and persistently struggling to defeat every enemy plot, scheme, attack, encroachment, raid, and sabotage activity, our southern armed forces and people have resolutely brought the war to his rear bases by combining armed struggle with political struggle, coordinating combat with mass uprisings, regaining and expanding the people's control by several degrees and in many forms in areas behind the enemy line, disturbing his rear bases, and gradually turning them into battlefields and our rear bases.

In past years, the north, the great rear base of the entire country, has been heavily protected and thus has had a great effect on our people's nationwide anti-U.S., national salvation undertaking. This has happened because the northern forces have been strengthened in every respect to cope with and defeat the enemy's war of destruction. But what is important is that the southern revolution has constantly matured, tirelessly developing its offensive strategy and scoring victory after victory on the great front line.

Fourth: Our Party has learned to build and consolidate the rear bases of the socialist north.

After the Dien Bien Phu victory, North Vietnam was entirely liberated, moving toward socialist construction and becoming a steadfast rear and base area for our people's nationwide revolutionary undertaking. This event marked a great turning point and a step forward in the process of building and developing the rear and base area of people's war in our country.

Since our Party assumed leadership over the Vietnamese people's struggle for independence and freedom, our people are—with half the country entirely liberated—advancing for the first time toward successfully building socialism, which is the most advanced social regime in our nation's several-thousand-year history, thus perfecting and consolidating this base area of our nationwide revolution.

Right after the successful anti-French resistance, our party stressed the need to consolidate and make the north solid and strong in every respect. According to the resolution of the Third Party Congress, the more strongly the north advanced toward socialism, the further all northern forces would be strengthened, thus benefiting the revolution for liberating the south, the development of our nationwide revolution, and the maintenance and consolidation of peace in Indochina and in the world. "The north is the common base area for our nation-wide revolution." *

The comprehensive consolidation and strengthening of all northern forces has further consolidated the north's national defense, a national defense of all the people built by the entire population and depending on the people's comprehensive strength to protect the people's interests, the revolutionary victory, and the socialist regime.

The views on the national defense of all the people were expressed for the first time in the resolution of the Twelfth Party Congress in 1957. This is the understanding of the concept of people's war and the task of defending the north and making it ready and able to smash every aggressive scheme of imperialism, while developing the effect of the north as a rear base of the nationwide revolution. This is a new step, under new conditions, in our Party's theory of building the rear and base of our people's war.

The building of the national defense of all the people in the north must be comprehensively conducted. To secure a steadfast, strong national defense of all the people, we must consolidate and strengthen the Party's leading role, the state of the proletarian dictatorship, the socialist regime, and, on the basis of the worker-peasant alliance, the unity and single-mindedness of the laboring people, workers, peasantry, and socialist intellectuals.

We must heighten socialist consciousness, patriotism, love for socialism, the spirit of collective rule, and the determination to reunify the country. We must satisfactorily carry out Party policies on mobilization and enlistment, toward wounded and sick combatants, toward dead heroes' families, toward soldiers' families, and so forth. And, on this basis, we must mobilize all our people in the struggle to step up production and build socialism, while being prepared to fight, and fight bravely, to defend the north, fulfill their obligations toward

* See the documents of the Congress, I, 32.—GIAP

the southern revolution, and to contribute to fulfilling international obligations.

The national defense by all the people of the north must rely on a sound socialist economy, and on this basis, economic construction may have great significance. While building our economy, we should coordinate it with national defense; we should associate peacetime requirements with those of wartime, immediate requirements with long range requirements. The coordination of our economy with national defense must be reflected not only in the over-all plan of the state but also in the plans of each branch—agricultural, industrial, communications, transport, and so forth; not only in the plans of the central echelons but also in those of the regional echelons, thus turning each step of economic development into a new step in developing national defense potentials by which, in case of war, we can quickly turn our peacetime economy into wartime economy. Moreover, we must have a correct, up-to-date line in changing economic [plans] according to the requirements of wartime, and we must hold fast the guideline that closely connects production with combat, to insure accelerated production, economic development, and services rendered to combat and the people's life in war.

The strength of national defense of all the people requires that the north be consolidated militarily. Military strength is not only that of a regular army but also that of the entire people, and it depends on the comprehensively steadfast new social regime, with the people's armed forces as the nucleus. The military construction task consists of: accelerating the arming and militarizing of the entire population; intensifying the building of the people's armed forces, including the three troop categories, the seasoned regular force, and the powerful reserve force; gradually building combat villages, hamlets, and wards; and intensifying the maintenance of security.

It is necessary to prepare the country in every respect and constantly to heighten the vigilant spirit and combat readiness of the armed forces and people so that every aggressive move and scheme of imperialism can be smashed. Moreover, it is necessary to stress the importance of every strategic area in national defense, to concentrate all forces on accelerating the comprehensive building and consolidation of particularly important areas, and to strengthen the leadership of the party and administration at all levels in consolidating national defense and army building.

The development of culture, education, science, technology, public health, physical training, sports, and so forth, is of great significance vis-à-vis the consolidation of national defense and the building of the economy and the army, especially the formation of new cadres and fighters possessing a high revolutionary consciousness, a fair cultural, scientific, and technical knowledge, and good health.

In sum, the entire national defense strength of the people of the north has been based on the comprehensive strength of the socialist regime and on achievements by the socialist revolution being carried on in the north. This strength has been tested in our people's struggle against the savage U.S. war of aggression perpetrated mainly by air power against the north. U.S. bombs and shells have not been able to subdue the northern people.

In this struggle, our entire people's spiritual and political solidarity has been strengthened more than ever before. Production has been maintained and developed. Communications and transportation have been guaranteed. Cultural, educational, and public-health activities have continued to develop. People's lives have been basically stabilized. The national defense forces have been consolidated and have developed by leaps and bounds.

The DRV is still proud, steadfast, and victorious, continuing to score successes for socialism and fulfilling all duties toward the south, the great front. Thus, the socialist regime has clearly displayed its definite superiority, and the entire northern people's national defense has displayed its great strength on various planes—political, organizational, material, technical, as well as spiritual, intellectual, and ethical.

Fifth: Our Party has learned to rely on the socialist camp, our board rear base area.

The Vietnamese revolution is an integral part of the world revolution and, since its early days, has enjoyed the latter's support. This support has been increasingly strengthened as our people carried on uprisings and wars. From being encircled by imperialism, we have advanced by firmly relying on socialism. Today, our people's anti-U.S., national salvation resistance is proceeding along with the socialist camp, which has developed by leaps and bounds, having a billion-plus population and strong economic and matchless national defense powers. This is the firm foundation to rely upon. It is our people's and the world peoples' steadfast bastion in the struggle for peace, national independence, democracy, and socialism.

Our people are in the vanguard of the struggle of the people of the world against imperialism, headed by the U.S. imperialists. The DRV is a component and the southern outpost of the socialist camp.

Therefore, while basically relying mainly on our own strength, we can and must strive to gain the sympathy, support, and assistance of the socialist camp in every aspect. This is a very important factor, which vigorously strengthens our people's fighting force in completely defeating the U.S. aggressors.

With an increasingly broad and strong rear, national and local bases, and relying on the generous capabilities of fraternal socialist countries, our people can develop our country's economic and military potential to the maximum and can grasp actual opportunities to push the anti-U.S., national salvation resistance toward complete victory.

PART 5. *To Apply Creatively the Formula for Waging War and Military Art of People's War.*

Our Party's military line holds that, to lead the people's war to victory, it is necessary to have a correct and creative military art and formula for waging war. To solve correctly and creatively the problem of mobilizing all our people to fight the enemy until victory, our Party has relied on the revolutionary nature and just cause of our people's national liberation war of national defense, on the concrete situation of the balance of power between ourselves and the enemy in our country and in the world, and on battlefield characteristics in our country.

Born out of the realities of our people's glorious struggle under Party leadership, a formula for waging war and a military art of great power and rich content have been shaped and perfected day by day. These are the formula for waging war and military art of people's war of the entire people and the comprehensive war of a small country with a small population struggling against large, aggressive imperialist armies. These are the formula and military art of waging military uprisings and revolutionary war, of resolutely attacking the enemy with both military and political forces, with [words indistinct] the protection and improvement of our own forces so that the more they fight, the stronger they become and the more victories they win, so that they can drive back the enemy step by step, annihilate him in large numbers, and advance toward complete victory.

Carrying out this formula and art, we must mainly rely on our own forces to develop the power of the just cause and the advantages of having the national liberation war of national defense fought in our own country; simultaneously, we must endeavor to win world sympathy and support and develop all the advantages of the present time, so as to create the combined power of people's war, defeat the enemy, and liberate and defend our country.

The following are the main points of our people's formula for waging war:

First: To wage a comprehensive war of all the people, and to associate military forces with political forces, armed struggle with political struggle, and armed uprisings with revolutionary war.

The main content of our Party's military line consists of mobilizing all the people to fight the enemy by waging armed uprisings and revolutionary war. Because the imperialists use their armed forces to invade our country and rule our people, we must arm all our people, organize our armed forces, and use armed struggle to defeat them. This is inevitable. However, to develop the greater power of all our people to defeat an enemy who has more troops and more powerful weapons but is engaging in an unjust, aggressive war and encountering many contradictions and weak points, we must fight him comprehensively, in the military field as well as in the political, economic, cultural, diplomatic, and other fields.

We must use various forms of struggle, including the most basic ones—that is, armed and political struggle. The combination of the armed forces with political forces, armed struggle with political struggle, and armed uprising with revolutionary war constitutes the main content of the formula of "waging a comprehensive war of all the people."

In our long history of building and protecting the country, our people, along with using the army to fight the aggressors, knew how to mobilize the people throughout the country to arise and fight, combining the army's combat with the people's uprising.

In shifting from political struggle to armed struggle in the effort to achieve the political objectives of the revolution, our people, under the Party's leadership, combined the armed forces with political forces, armed struggle with political struggle, and the masses' uprising with armed forces' combat.

Armed struggle is an aspect of basic struggle, directly playing a decisive role in annihilating the enemy's military forces. Along with the task of annihilating the enemy's militant forces, the armed struggle is also duty-bound to protect the people, to win them over, to combine with political struggle, and to support the revolutionary masses in conducting their political struggle, in arising, in gaining the right to rule, and in scoring the greatest successes for the revolution. The more fiercely the war develops, the more important the armed struggle.

At a time when the aggressors have intensified the use of armed forces to invade our country and enslave our people, the use of armed struggle to counter their armed aggression has become increasingly important and imperative. It is necessary to annihilate the enemy's military forces, to doom all his military strategies, and to defeat him militarily so as to score success for the resistance.

Political struggle is an aspect of basic struggle. It is always a base on which armed struggle can develop, and it is also a formula for attacking the enemy. The purpose of political struggle is to mobilize and organize the people, to lead the people in the struggle against the enemy, from lowest to highest levels, to expose and doom every deceitful enemy trick, to disperse and weaken his military forces, to confuse his rear base area, and to protect the people's livelihood and production and the revolutionary bases.

During the uprising and war, the political struggle has incessantly developed into armed struggle and has closely combined with it in scoring the greatest successes for the revolution. The people's political forces have advanced from the ordinary aspects of political struggle toward conducting an armed uprising under definite conditions and cooperating with the armed forces in directly deciding the formation of the revolutionary administration.

The combination of political forces and armed forces, political struggle with armed combat, and armed uprising with revolutionary war is of a universal nature and is a law governing revolutionary violence in our country. Our people have cleverly made use of this combination, adjusting it to each concrete situation.

Political force now plays the main role of a prop—associating political struggle with armed struggle to advance toward a nationwide armed uprising. Military force now plays the main role in the war of all the people—in association with political force—associating armed combat with political struggle and fighting with uprising, using armed struggle as the main form of struggle in carrying out a protracted revolutionary war. Military force is now associated with political force in conducting armed struggle along with political struggle and armed uprising along with revolutionary war.

In the general uprising of August, 1945, our people's strong mass forces, supported by the liberation troops, resorted to widespread armed uprising to regain administrative power in urban and rural areas.

The August Revolution succeeded essentially because our people's political force seized in time the most favorable opportunity to start the uprising to win administrative power for the state. But the revolution would not have succeeded promptly if our Party had not before [carefully] built the armed forces and vast base areas as a prop for political force and the political struggle movement, and if it had not quickly launched the armed uprising when the conditions were ripe.*

In the anti-French resistance, all our people rose up to fight the enemy, using the people's armed forces as the nucleus. In the coordination of armed struggle with political struggle, armed struggle was the main form of struggle. The armed forces conducted guerrilla warfare and, on this basis, moved toward regular warfare. In this process, they constantly and closely coordinated their combat activities with political struggle and the partial uprising of the masses behind the enemy lines.

Whereas the enemy had achieved the old colonialism, the revolutionary masses in many urban and rural areas resolutely conducted face-to-face, multiform struggles against terrorism, massacre, strafing, pillage, military conscription, and forced labor, demanding the return of their husbands and

* Political report by the Party's Central Committee to the Third Party Congress on September 5, 1960.—GIAP

sons, motivating puppet troops to join the revolution, coordinating combat with military proselytizing, annihilating spies and villains, staging partial uprisings, overthrowing the enemy's basic administration in the countryside, and so forth.

The present revolutionary war in South Vietnam is coordination, at a new level and under new historical conditions, between armed and political forces, between armed and political struggles, and between armed uprising and revolutionary war to overthrow the neo-colonialist, aggressive war. This is a very great stride in the development of the comprehensive war of the entire people.

All the 14 million southern people are rushing toward the front line, attacking the U.S. aggressive troops and the puppet army and administration in the military, political, and troop-proselytizing spheres, conducting widespread uprisings in war, and coordinating political struggle with armed struggle and armed uprising with revolutionary war.

The military proselytizing task, aimed at enlightening puppet troops and attracting them to the revolutionary side, has become a strategic offensive spearhead of the revolutionary movement to achieve the "worker-peasant-troop alliance" slogan of the southern revolution.

In war, on the basis of a widespread struggle movement and with the coordination of the people's armed forces in attacks against enemy troops, the mass-uprising movement can be launched even more vigorously on certain occasions. An uprising can help widen the terrain, increase war forces, and accelerate the war, whereas the war can ripen the conditions for uprising and stimulate the steady expansion of the uprising.

Even though uprising and war are different from each other, as Lenin remarked, they cannot be separated and are difficult to distinguish.*

In the comprehensive war of our entire people, along with the fundamental military and political struggles, economic

* *Strategy and Tactics in the October Revolution,* See That edition, p. 269.—GIAP

struggle also plays a very important role, especially when we have bases and rear base areas, when the liberation war is developed and broadened, or when we carry on a national defense war.

Along with motivating a war economy, we must resolutely carry on economic struggle against the enemy, coordinate political and military struggles with economic struggle to harass the enemy's economic foundations, to drive his economy into disorder and stalemate, to safeguard and develop our economy in wartime, to safeguard the people's lives, to boost production and saving vigorously, to defeat all the enemy's maneuvers that harass our economy, and so on.

Second: To quarter steadfastly in rural areas, to carry on people's war in mountains, lowlands, and cities, closely coordinating attacks, with adequate tactics, against the enemy in these strategic areas.

By skillfully coordinating armed force with political force, armed struggle with political struggle, and uprisings with war, we can develop to a high degree the enormous strength of the entire nation, which is determined to fight and to attack the enemy in all strategic areas, from mountains to plains and from rural areas to cities.

To attack the enemy in all three strategic areas—mountains, lowlands, and cities—with adequate tactics is a very important point in the way we carry out our revolutionary war. Therefore, one of the strategic problems of revolutionary war in our country is to determine the respective positions of rural areas and cities, to quarter steadfastly in rural areas, to attack the enemy in rural areas as well as in cities, to coordinate closely the attacks against the enemy throughout the three strategic areas, to coordinate armed struggle with political struggle and uprisings with war, according to the concrete conditions of each area. We must also focus guidance in this or that area to accord with existing conditions and the different periods of armed uprisings or our revolutionary war.

During World War II and in the period preceding the August, 1945, general uprising, the revolution in our country

was carried out primarily in the rural and mountainous areas
in the form of limited guerrilla warfare and limited uprisings.
However, the revolutionary movement in the vast rural and
delta areas and in the urban areas continued to develop in
various suitable forms of struggle. As a result, when great
opportunities presented themselves, our people won the
greatest victory in the August Revolution by insuring coordination between the urban and rural revolutionary movements and between our political and armed forces and by
staging timely, victorious general uprisings in both the urban
and rural areas.

Following in the footsteps of the allied forces, the French
expeditionary corps again invaded our country. The anti-
French resistance initially broke out in the urban areas. Subsequently, for a long period of time, our people's anti-French
war, in which armed combat was the main form of struggle,
was waged mainly in the rural areas. But our political struggle
and armed activities in the rural areas, in the enemy's rear
base areas, and in the urban areas, also developed in close
coordination with the armed struggle in the rural, delta, and
mountainous areas.

The 1959–60 spontaneous uprising in the southern revolution broke out in the rural areas and, subsequently, developed
into a guerrilla war, in which our people coordinated their
attacks against the enemy in the rural areas with the urban
political movement. Specifically, from 1963 to early 1965, the
armed struggle and uprisings, aimed at destroying strategic
hamlets in the rural areas in coordination with the urban
mass movement, enabled our people to acquire a great combined strength that defeated the U.S. imperialists' special war.

During the 1965–67 period, the southern armed forces and
people continued to develop their strategic, offensive position,
vigorously attacking the enemy in all three strategic areas—
the mountainous-rural, rural-delta, and urban areas—through
armed and political struggles, coordinating their armed and
political struggles in varying degrees and in different operational areas. The rural, mountainous, and delta areas were

the main battlefields on which armed combat and uprisings were coordinated. Meanwhile, in the urban areas, the political struggle developed, and armed activities were carried out to a certain degree.

Through their first general offensive in 1968, the southern armed forces and people acquired an offensive position from which they have launched concerted attacks and staged widespread uprisings in both the urban and rural areas, winning increasingly great victories.

As pointed out in the preceding analysis, the rural and urban areas are both important in the armed uprisings and revolutionary war in our country, although they perform different functions. By coordinating armed and political struggles, combining combat with uprisings to appropriate degrees and in various strategic operational areas, maintaining a firm foothold in the rural areas, regarding the rural areas as firm battlegrounds, developing the urban revolutionary forces, and regarding the urban areas as crucial operational areas, we can vigorously attack the enemy in both the rural and urban areas and in all three strategic areas, and compel him to spread his forces out over a wide area.

We can also coordinate our activities in various operational areas, continuously attack the enemy everywhere and at any time, sow chaos in his rear base, and direct powerful blows at him. We can defeat the enemy in a protracted war. We also possess conditions to create opportunities, bide for time, direct timely, vigorous blows at the enemy, and win increasingly great victories.

In people's war in our country, only by attacking the enemy in all three strategic areas can we successfully develop the enormous strength of all our revolutionary forces—whose main-force army consists of the workers and peasants—develop the strength originating in the coordination between armed and political struggles and between the war and uprisings, and thereby achieve the greatest victories for the revolution.

When we have a perfect nation with its urban and rural

areas—and when our country's industry is increasingly developed—in building the people's national defense or in waging a national defense war, the positions of the urban and rural areas will not be as completely identical as they have been. The coordination between the rural and urban areas in a national defense war displays distinct features that differ from those of a national liberation war. For example, people's war to counteract the war of destruction against the north has given [us] some experience. In this situation, the coordination between rural and urban areas is a matter of rule in comprehensively developing the strength of our regime and country in order to defeat the enemy.

Third: To understand thoroughly the strategic-offensive ideology in armed uprisings and in the revolutionary war.

By mobilizing all the people to fight the aggressors and by coordinating armed and political struggles in every strategic operational area, we have mustered an enormous strength in the people's war with which to attack the enemy.

Revolution is an offensive. The history of our people's forty-year-long, Party-led struggle as a whole has been a process during which our people have [routed] the enemy resolutely, continuously, and victoriously. Arising from domination to topple the oppressive yoke of imperialism and its lackeys, and to regain and maintain their rule over their country, our people have thoroughly and profoundly understood the strategic-offensive ideology of the revolution.

Uprisings represent an offensive. Revolutionary war, viewed in its whole process, represents an offensive. At times and at certain places, the revolutionary war may be in a defensive position. But this defensive position is only partial and temporary, [lasting only] until conditions have been created for resuming the offensive.

Since 1940, moving from political struggle into armed struggle, our people have been determined to attack the enemy. Especially since March, 1945, our people have waged partial uprisings to overthrow enemy administrative organs in vast areas, along with attacking the enemy everywhere by using adequate forms of struggle. Our people also have un-remittingly broadened partial uprisings and local guerrilla warfare, have vigorously added to the ferment of political struggle throughout the country, and have advanced toward the glorious August general uprising to carry out the most comprehensive, vehement, determined, and opportune offensive to overthrow the enemy's administration and regain nationwide power for the people.

Soon after the successful August Revolution, the French colonialists again invaded our country. Our Party launched the entire people's national salvation resistance. In the early days of the nationwide resistance, when we faced the aggressive army's temporary strength, we aimed at preserving our main force by avoiding disadvantageous battles and retreating to a certain limit,* while actively trying to attack the enemy everywhere and to attack and destroy the enemy's separate elements;† then, aiming at driving the enemy into the defensive,‡ we launched guerrilla warfare, deeply penetrated the enemy's rear base area, and turned it into our vanguard. We have gradually intensified our offensive by guerrilla as well as regular warfare.

After the border operation in 1950, following local counterattacks, we advanced toward carrying out our great strategic counterattack of winter-spring 1953–54, the climax of which was the glorious Dien Bien Phu operation that successfully ended the resistance and liberated half of the nation.

In the southern part of our country, during the fight against the U.S. imperialists' extremely cruel neo-colonialist ruling yoke, the southern revolution shifted to a strategic offensive position through the 1959–60 general uprising movement; later, it tirelessly developed its offensive position, enlarged the masses' phased uprising and political struggle, developed guerrilla warfare, and proceeded from guerrilla fighting to concentrated fighting, simultaneously applying military and

* Nikolai Lenin, *Complete Works,* XXVII, 54–55.—GIAP

† Excerpt from the resolution of the Second Cadre Conference, April 3–6, 1967.—GIAP

‡ Central instruction of October 15, 1947.—GIAP

political formulas, and dooming the U.S. imperialists' special war strategy. When the U.S. imperialists employed hundreds of thousands of their modern military men to invade our country directly, our army and people did not hesitate for a moment but resolutely and firmly maintained their initiative, continuously attacking the enemy, carrying on their strategy of attacking him in the limited war, and frustrating every enemy plot.

The early Mau Than spring general offensive and concerted uprisings vigorously pushed forward the strategic-offensive position of our army and people, thus bringing the development of the war to a new phase. In short, in the entire process of conducting their uprisings and war, our army and people have incessantly developed the proletariat's thoroughly revolutionary spirit and have constantly and thoroughly grasped the "offensive-strategy" ideology of the revolution and revolutionary war.

The present offensive ideology of our party, armed forces, and people is not disassociated from our traditional national military ideology. In our national history, generally speaking, the victorious uprisings and national liberation was led by the Trung sisters, Ly Bon, Trieu Quang, [name missing], Le Loi, and Nguyen Trai, representing various processes of continuous offensive aimed at toppling the foreign feudal ruling yoke.

The victorious wars of national defense led by Ly Thuong Kiet, Tran Huong Dao, and Nguyen Hue were made up of various necessary defensive phases and strategic withdrawals at the outset; but, in these wars, the prominent ideology constantly remained the offensive ideology with glorious counter-offensives on river [name indistinct], in Van Kiep, on Bach Dang River, in Dong Da, and elsewhere.

How could our people resolutely and continuously counter-attack an enemy possessing economic and military potential-ities far greater than ours and drive him into a passive, defensive position and defeat him? Our army and people, who conducted armed uprisings and the revolutionary war, possess a very high offensive ideology. The offensive constitutes an ideological basis of the Vietnamese revolutionary strategy and offensive. It originates from the thoroughly revolutionary nature of our Party's political and military lines, from the ardent patriotism and the extremely creative and resolute combativity of our Vietnamese people, who have fought for independence, freedom, and socialism.

Our offensive ability is closely associated with our assessment of the characteristics and development of the balance of forces between us and the enemy in the fight between the two sides. Our enemy has not only strong points but also weak points—very many basic weak points. Our people never have weak points. They have strong points—very many basic strong points. This is the strength of an entire people who stand up to defend their country. This is the strength of the just war in the present era. We can absolutely develop our strong points and attack the enemy's weak points.

The great offensive ability of our army and people is also closely associated with our leadership over people's war and with various forms of struggle coupled with unique and creative combat methods of people's war in our country. Because we know how to attack the enemy comprehensively, through armed and political struggles, combining [armed] uprising, guerrilla warfare, and conventional war, our army and people have, therefore, developed all our capabilities for attacking the enemy. Because we know how to devise creatively various appropriate and highly effective methods, our armed forces have developed to a high degree the offensive strength needed to attack and annihilate the enemy.

Fourth: To apply the strategy of protracted war while striving to create opportunities and gain time to score even greater victories.

Our nation's history is filled with successful uprisings and wars that defeated stronger adversaries who had subjugated our people or invaded our country.

The time for staging these uprisings and wars depends on many concrete conditions, especially on the balance of forces between ourselves and the enemy and on our part of conducting the war.

Some wars ended unsuccessfully within a relatively short time, while some national liberation wars were protracted ones. Under the Tran Dynasty, three resistance movements against the Chinese invaders lasted thirty years, but each of these successful resistances took place within only a few months. Hero Nguyen Hue's marvelously fast troop movement won a great victory within a very short time. Meanwhile, the liberation war led by Le Loi and Nguyen Trai ended victoriously after ten years of hard struggle. For this reason, our people inherently possess a tradition of persistent resistance, an art of defeating the enemy in protracted wars, and experience in creating and taking advantage of all favorable conditions to win success within a relatively short time.

At present, under an advanced political regime and with a steadfast solidarity bloc of all the people led by the Party, we can develop highly all the material and spiritual strength of our people and our country. Moreover, we enjoy the valuable aid of our fraternal socialist countries and the sympathy and support of progressives throughout the world.

Because our country was a semi-feudalist colony and is small, underpopulated, and economically underdeveloped, and because our enemy is by nature a very stubborn, perfidious imperialist, whose country is vast and populous and who possesses a greater economic and military potential and a large, modern army, there exists not only an imbalance of numerical strength and population but also a great imbalance of technical equipment.

Under these circumstances, we must have time gradually to weaken and exterminate enemy forces, to restrict his strength and aggravate his weaknesses, gradually to strengthen and develop our forces, and to overcome our deficiencies. Thus, the more the enemy fights, the weaker he will become, and the more we fight, the stronger we will become. For this reason, the strategy of people's war is a protracted one. The more we fight, the stronger we will become, the more numerous will be our victories, and the nearer we will move toward final victory.

The realities of scores of years of relentless struggle by our people and their glorious victories have proved the correctness of our Party's protracted-war strategy. In general, the process of a protracted struggle is that of successively attacking the enemy, gradually repelling him, partially overthrowing him, defeating every one of his strategic schemes, gradually scoring victories, and moving toward defeating him completely.

The length of the war depends on changes in the balance of forces between us and the enemy and on the war leadership of both sides. Our people's war experience has shown that, in the process of a long war, when the war moves from one phase to another, there often are fluctuations by leaps and bounds as the result either of our efforts, of the enemy's mistakes, or of effective objective conditions.

The rule of development in every movement process is to progress from step-by-step to leap-and-bound developments. Uprisings and war are fierce competitions, life-or-death struggles between us and the enemy. Therefore, this rule appears more clearly in uprisings and war.

In uprisings and war, if we know how to develop highly our subjective efforts, to take maximum advantage of all advantageous objective conditions, to develop the enemy's weaknesses and mistakes and to turn them into profit, to create excellent tactics, to aim at right targets, to look for opportunities, to deal heavy blows, to gain great military victories, and to coordinate skillfully armed struggle with political struggle and military operations with uprisings, we shall be able to create favorable conditions for carrying out more important leaps and bounds to gain great successes in war. Therefore, on the basis of persistent counterattack, we must always try to do our utmost in every way to create opportunities, to gain time, and to score greater successes.

Fifth: To coordinate the annihilation of the enemy with the gaining and maintaining of administrative power for the people, actively to destroy the enemy's forces, and to maintain and improve our forces, so that the more we fight, the stronger we become.

The fundamental problem of every revolution is that of government. The fundamental problem of every war is that of annihilating the enemy's armed forces. Our war is a revolutionary war. In using war as a means of struggle for gaining administrative power, we must aim at annihilating the enemy's armed forces as well as at solving the problem of smashing the enemy's government and regaining administrative power for the people.

During the uprisings and revolutionary wars in our country, our people have closely coordinated armed struggles with political struggle, wars with uprisings. Therefore, there have been the people's armed forces' military actions to annihilate the enemy as well as the masses' uprisings to regain administrative power. The problem of the people's gaining the right to rule is that of toppling the enemy's administration and of seizing the administration for the people, at varying degrees, in conformity with various existing conditions and in definite zones, in the long process of offensive against the enemy.

The exercise of this right to rule can be manifested in varying degrees and in various forms, with the aim of creating necessary conditions for attacking the enemy through various appropriate forms in the protracted fight against him. In the process of attacking the enemy, the armed forces' annihilation of the enemy must be closely associated with the masses' uprising to gain the right to rule. We must annihilate the enemy in order to support the masses in arising and gaining the right to rule.

It is necessary to arise and gain the right to rule to acquire more operational theaters and offensive forces with which to annihilate the enemy. Therefore, combining the annihilation of the enemy with the gaining and firm protection of the people's right to rule is a law for winning victory that governs armed uprising and revolutionary war in our country. In the general uprising in August, 1945, the masses' uprising to gain the right to rule and, especially, the administration, was a main task. However, the masses at that time had to be supported and backed by the armed forces that were charged with annihilating the enemy.

In the anti-French resistance, the armed forces' use of armed struggle to annihilate the enemy was a main task, but the masses also arose; they destroyed the puppet administration, eliminated villains, seized the administration in areas in the enemy's rear, and built, consolidated, and developed guerrilla zones and bases in the midst of areas under the enemy's control. Our army and people also widely and actively built and consolidated free zones, built and consolidated the people's administration, defeated enemy counteroffensives and offensives, and firmly protected our free zones.

In the present southern revolutionary war, the problem of combining the annihilation of the enemy with the gaining and firm protection of the people's right to rule has developed further. The southern liberation armed forces have actively attacked and annihilated the enemy, at the same time supporting the people's political struggles and uprisings to gain the right to rule. The masses' political forces have actively attacked the enemy through appropriate forms and have coordinated with the armed forces in conducting phased uprisings to topple the administration at basic levels, to gain the right to rule in varying degrees, to put together the revolutionary administration in one form or another, and to create more favorable conditions for the armed forces in annihilating the enemy.

In the liberated areas, it is necessary to fight actively to protect the people and to build and consolidate the people's right to rule in the political and economic fields. In order to meet the requirement of the law governing the combination of the annihilation of the enemy with the people's gaining and protection of the right to rule, we must understand thoroughly the ideology of actively annihilating enemy forces and of protecting and strengthening our forces.

Annihilating enemy forces means annihilating his military

and political forces. It means annihilating not only the foreign aggressors' military and political forces but also annihilating or distintegrating the lackeys' military and political forces. Protecting and strengthening our forces means protecting and strengthening the forces of the army and the people and the military, political, and economic forces.

Only through keeping a firm hold on and correctly applying the rules governing the association between annihilating enemy troops and regaining the right of the people to rule and only through fully understanding the necessity of annihilating the enemy forces and preserving and improving our own forces, can we carry out the motto, "The more we fight, the stronger we become, the more we fight, the more victories we win," make our forces increasingly mature, enlarge our operational areas day by day, develop the comprehensively offensive position of the revolutionary war day by day, and advance toward defeating the enemy's military forces and strategies, crushing his administration at all levels, and regaining all authority for the people.

In the war of national defense, we must annihilate the enemy's military forces in order to preserve our national sovereignty. We must actively regain authority in the areas under the enemy's temporary control and actively associate the annihilation of enemy troops with the preservation and improvement of our own forces. Carrying out the motto "The more we fight the stronger we become" is a very important strategic problem in the national defense war as well as in the national liberation war.

Sixth: To rely mainly on one's own forces and simultaneously endeavor to win over international support.

This is also a rule governing the success of the Vietnamese revolution and revolutionary war in our present era. This rule marks a new step in the development of our Party's war-leadership art compared to the previous historical phases. It reflects the view that regards revolution as the work of the masses. It reflects our Party's unshakable confidence in the strength of our nation and people.

Moreover, it reflects the view that regards the Vietnamese revolution as part of the world revolution, continually associating our revolution with the world people's revolutionary movement.

It tends to develop the advantages of this era in order to achieve the success of our revolution and revolutionary war, thus enabling our people to make positive contributions to the revolutionary work of other people throughout the world.

Our Party holds that the success of our revolutionary war mainly depends upon internal causes—the correct line of our Party, the efforts of our troops and people on the battlefield, the political, moral, and material capacities of our people, and the favorable weather, terrain, and popular support of the war of national liberation or war of national defense that is developing in our country.

Therefore, with the highest sense of political responsibility toward the nation's destiny and a spirit of self-reliance, our Party has creatively applied Marxism-Leninism to the situation of our country to set forth a revolutionary line and the line to carry out correctly and independently the revolutionary war, to mobilize, organize, and employ all the strength of our nation and people to achieve victories.

We have thoroughly understood that the Vietnamese people must undertake by themselves alone—rather than asking other people to do it for them—the resistance for regaining the Vietnamese fatherland's independence and freedom. Our people's great victories have been mainly and primarily the results of the sacrifices and extremely heroic struggle by all our Party, army, and people. In the August Revolution, in the resistance against the French colonialists, and in the present resistance against the U.S. imperialists and their henchmen, our people have arisen by themselves alone to fight and defeat powerful enemies and have fought for a long time in a situation in which our country is surrounded on all sides by the imperialists.

These great victories clearly prove the great strength of our people, who have firmly held to the self-reliance principle.

These great victories also cannot be separated from the support and assistance of the revolutionary people throughout the world. The world revolutionary movement has created objective and very favorable conditions for the revolution and the revolutionary war in our country. Although our country is still surrounded by the imperialists, we are not isolated from the fraternal socialist countries; thus, we have continued to enjoy, directly or indirectly, [the support of] the fraternal socialist countries and the revolutionary people throughout the world.

Due to our Party's correct policy of international solidarity, our people have gained the strong and broad sympathy and assistance of our friends on the five continents. At present, the socialist camp has become a decisive factor for the development of the society of mankind and the movements that struggle fervently for peace, national independence, democracy, and socialism in the world.

The [world?] imperialists headed by the U.S. imperialists are under attack everywhere. Our people should and can develop fully the advantages of the time to create a strong posture and strength in the war to defeat the aggressors. International assistance can develop its effects only through the objective efforts of our people and Party. Therefore, although we attach great consideration to international assistance, we should always rely on our own efforts and closely associate relying on our own efforts with the strong development of international assistance.

PART 6. *To Apply Creatively the Formula for Waging War and Military Art of People's War: In the Formula for Waging War, the Military Art Is an Extremely Important Component Whose Task Is to Solve the Problems of Armed Struggle in the People's War. Our Military Art Reflects the Laws of Revolutionary Armed Struggle in General and of Revolutionary Armed Struggle in Our Country in Particular. Due to the Characteristics of the Revolutionary Armed Struggle in Our Country, Our Military Art Also Reflects the Close Relationships Between Armed Struggle and Political Struggle and Between Revolutionary War and Armed Insurrection.*

Our military art correctly determines the organic relationship and interaction among strategy, campaign, and tactics, which are the components that make up this art, and it correctly determines the role of each component.

Strategy is the main component. A correct military strategy creates the fundamental condition for the favorable fulfillment of the tasks in campaign and combat. Conversely, only by successfully solving problems relating to campaign and tactics and successfully fulfilling all the tasks of combat on the battlefield do we have a basis for achieving the objectives set forth by military strategy.

Our military art is always deeply imbued with the basic content, viewpoints, and thoughts of the Party's military line and of the formula for carrying out a revolutionary war as presented above.

First: Proceeding from the basic content the Party's military line—that is, the whole country of one mind, the entire people's fight against the bandits—our military art is first and foremost the military art of the entire people fighting against the bandits. As President Ho pointed out in his appeal to the entire nation to carry out resistance in December, 1946: Every Vietnamese, regardless of sex or age, regardless of religion, party affiliation, or nationality, must stand up and fight the French colonialists in order to save the fatherland. Let anyone who has a gun use the gun and anyone who has a sword use the sword. Those who have no swords should use picks and sticks. Everyone must exert efforts to fight against the colonialists and save the country.

Our military art guides the fighting activities of the armed forces and, at the same time, guides the military activities of the people, who stand up with weapons in their hands to fight the enemy, overthrow the enemy's administrative power, and cause his armed forces to disintegrate. In line with this requirement, our military art must correctly determine the tasks of the armed forces and armed struggle in our people's all-out war.

Parallel with the annihilation of the enemy's military forces, armed struggle should create favorable conditions for building and developing a military base, should step up the political struggle of the masses, and should push forward the work of military recruitment, creating conditions for the masses to rise up to wrest back their sovereign right.

On the other hand, the armed struggle should make full use of the victories of the political struggle and of the work of military recruitment, so as to develop the military offensive and thus annihilate more of the enemy. To do so, the armed struggle should grasp the task and requirements of the political struggle in each region and actively meet these requirements. For this reason, closely coordinating military affairs with politics, fighting with military recruitment, and annihilating the enemy military forces along with launching the masses to wrest back their sovereign right, have for a long time now become the guiding combat principles of our armed forces.

In people's war, the people's armed forces, comprising the three categories of troops, are the core of the entire people's struggle against the bandits. To develop the strength of all the people, our military art should guide the fighting activities of the main force troops and should, at the same time, guide the fighting activities of the regional armed forces. Only by closely coordinating the fighting activities of the main-force troops, regional troops, and self-defense militia, coordinating guerrilla attack with concentrated attack, and coordinating small offensive with medium and large offensive, are we able to maintain firmly and advance victoriously the revolutionary war of all the people.

Second: Our military art is permeated with the idea of active attack on the enemy. It is mainly the art of attack. Imbued with the strategic idea of offensive in the revolutionary war, let us in our armed struggle actively attack the enemy in a resolute, continuous, and thorough manner, with all forces and weapons, in all forms, on all scales, everywhere, and at all times.

Our military art, being an art of all the people fighting the bandits and being capable of developing its strong points and striking at the enemy's shortcomings, is fully able to create a balance of forces that favors us in our attacks on the enemy, and is able to increase the offensive from a small attack to a big one and from a localized attack to a generalized attack.

In the adoption of different forms of fighting, including offensive and defensive, major attention is given to offense. There are places and times when we must carry out defense to support the offense, but the defense is merely a function to insure that the majority of our forces carry out the offensive; it is a temporary measure to create conditions for moving to the offensive. Each and every defensive task must be carried out with an active and determined spirit to seize the initiative constantly in attacking the enemy.

Permeated with the idea of offense, our military art emphasizes developing political superiority and the valiancy and resourcefulness of the Vietnamese people, who have a high degree of political consciousness, a spirit of close solidarity, and a tradition of courage and talent in strategy. Our military art develops the strong points of the new social regime and the just struggle taking place in our land. It fully utilizes all weapons, from rudimentary to modern ones, and establishes many highly efficient combat measures to defeat aggressor armies that in number and in technique are strong but that have many fundamental shortcomings in politics, morale, and even military affairs.

By constantly raising political consciousness, developing human bravery and intelligence to a high degree, correctly solving the relationship between man and weapons, and giving priority to the human element—the political and moral aspects—while also attaching importance to the weapon element —the material and technical aspects—our military art has created for our armed forces and people extremely great capabilities with which to attack the enemy.

Third: Our military art is the art of using a small force to fight a big force. The realistic situation of war of national liberation and patriotic war, at present as well as in the past, has posed to our people—a people whose population is not very big and whose territory is not very large—the strategic requirement of defeating enemies who have large armies and economic and military potentialities many times greater than ours. Confronted with this strategic requirement, our forefathers, to achieve victory, created the art of using a weak force to fight a strong enemy, using a small force to fight a bigger one, and [waging short battles] to win [protracted wars]. On many occasions, they completely annihilated huge enemy aggressor armies.

In the present situation of the balance of forces between us and the enemy, particularly in the number of effectives and technical equipment, to defeat the enemy, we must be all the more determined in the practice of using a small force to fight a bigger one. Imbued with the strategic idea of using a small force to fight a bigger one in our campaign and combat, we must know how to use a small force to fight a bigger one, at the same time knowing how to concentrate our forces rationally when we must fight the enemy and annihilate him.

Using a small force to fight a bigger one means using a small force to win big victories. It means carrying out not only small offensives but also medium and big offensives. Our ancestors, using a small force to fight a bigger one, wiped out in one battle thousands and thousands of the enemy.

The South Vietnamese armed forces and people, using a small force to fight a bigger one in their anti-U.S. resistance for national salvation, have used a small but well-trained force to annihilate or put out of action, in one battle, regiments and brigades of the enemy, or to destroy dozens of his aircraft, hundreds of his armored vehicles, and thousands of tons of his matériel and ammunition.

Practicing the concept of using a small force to fight a bigger one to counter the enemy who carried out the war of destruction in North Vietnam, our air defense and air forces in many battles knew how to employ small militia forces, anti-aircraft troops, and the air force to cope victoriously with the numerous air forces of the enemy, as well as how to down enemy aircraft with a limited amount of ammunition.

When concentrating our forces, we must know how to use them in the most rational way, creating the greatest fighting power so that we can overwhelm the enemy and attack continuously to annihilate him and attain the objective, while using as few of our forces as possible. A very fundamental requirement of the thinking that guides our combat performance is that by organizing appropriate forces, by developing valiant and resourceful behavior, by creating a favorable fighting position and a good fighting technique, and by creating and maintaining conditions that prevent the development of the enemy's power and effective offensive fighting and that cause enemy forces to accept our blows passively, we must attain the advantage in each battle of fighting the enemy from a position of strength, of achieving superiority, and creating a combined fighting strength greater than that of the enemy, so as to annihilate him.

Fourth: Our military art is deeply imbued with the idea of actively annihilating the enemy.

Developing the offensive concept of using a small force to fight a bigger one, we must achieve the primary objective of all battlefield activity, namely, wiping out the enemy's military forces. In war, along with wearing out and annihilating small portions of the enemy in widespread guerrilla actions, the most concentrated armed forces—particularly the main-force units—must resolutely wipe out increasingly more important segments of the enemy forces. They must resolutely attain the requirement of completely annihilating increasingly larger units of the enemy, capturing prisoners of war, seizing weapons, and mastering the battlefield, while sustaining few losses on our side.

The enemy's military force consists of his numerical strength, means of waging war, and rear bases. His numerical strength is the most important component, but the means of waging war and the rear bases are also very important components in the fighting power of an imperialist army. That is why, at the same time that we annihilate of the enemy's strength, we must destroy his means of waging war and his rear bases, making sure to wipe out the most important parts of his strength, means of waging war, and his rear bases.

In conjunction with annihilating the enemy's military forces, our army should coordinate with our political forces to smash the enemy's administrative power at various levels, to shatter his forces of oppression in various regions of the country, and to bring about the disintegration of his armed civil organizations.

By wiping out or causing the disintegration of the enemy's military and political forces and his main and regional forces, by annihilating his strength and destroying his means of waging war and his rear bases, and by obliterating both his regular and his first-line forces, we shall weaken the enemy from all sides.

With a certain strength, we may be able to deal the most telling blows to the enemy, causing him the heaviest losses, restricting his strong points, and defeating his strong fighting methods, thereby vigorously contributing to our people's all-out resistance. This is also the way to determine our objectives rationally, so that we can develop the strength of all of our forces and effectively defeat an enemy who had a large army and many modern technical means.

Fifth: Our military art is the art of fighting the enemy in an active, resolute, lively, resourceful, creative, secret, and unexpected manner.

With great motivation to attack and annihilate the enemy, our armed forces and people, in their armed struggle, are constantly upholding the spirit of actively looking for the enemy to fight him and are fighting him resolutely. We must actively attack enemy troops, attack them on our own initiative, and attack them resolutely; and we must always maintain our initiative and always fight the enemy from a position of strength.

To defeat a modern aggressor army with large numerical strength, with enormous firepower and great mobility, an army that is at the same time stubborn and perfidious, we must fight him in a spirit of daring and with a great determination and perseverance in our struggle, until he is completely annihilated. Each wartime combat action of our armed forces and people has been imbued with this view of fighting inherent in the Vietnamese revolutionary military art. At the same time, application of this concept of fighting has occurred in a very lively manner and has changed according to each stage of development of each war and according to existing conditions relative to the enemy, to us, to our people, and to the terrain and weather pertaining to each battlefield.

Creative resourcefulness is an important requirement of our military art. Only by developing to a high degree creative resourcefulness on the basis of the proletariat's thoroughgoing revolutionary spirit, ardent patriotism, and love for socialism can we successfully materialize the concept of the offensive and the use of a small force to defeat a larger one in every circumstance.

In our art of fighting against the bandits, both in the past and at present, secrecy and surprise are outstanding points. Possessing a strong determination to annihilate the bandits, having an intelligent and creative approach, knowing how to rely on the people, and having a high consciousness of organization and discipline, our armed forces always act unpredictably in fighting the enemy, unpredictably in their direction of attack, their target, time, use of force, scope of attack, manner of attack, and so forth.

While disagreeing with the assertion of imperialism that surprise is the factor that determines victory or defeat in war, we highly appreciate the effect of the element of surprise in annihilating the enemy. Carrying out surprise attacks on the enemy strategically as well as tactically, our armed forces and people have scored great victories in their war for national salvation.

Permeated with the above viewpoints and thoughts, the military art of the Vietnam people's war has successfully solved many problems of strategy, campaign, and tactics in accordance with different current conditions.

(1) First of all, our military art consists of stepping up the fighting of the three categories of troops as the core of the fight of all the people against the bandits, carrying out guerrilla and regular war, and closely coordinating guerrilla war with regular war.

If coordination of the armed forces with the political forces, armed struggle with political struggle, and armed insurrection with revolutionary war is the main content of the formula for carrying out the all-out war of all the people, then in the field of armed struggle and in the waging of guerrilla and regular wars, the coordination of guerrilla war with regular war is the most fundamental part of the art of sending all the people headlong into the fight against the bandits in our country.

Guerrilla warfare is a form of armed struggle by the masses of the people. Due to the characteristics of people's war in our country, where the whole nation is of one mind and all the people fight against the bandits, guerrilla war develops in a widespread, powerful, and varied manner. The different strata of our people and the various nationalities in our country adopt guerrilla warfare to fight the enemy directly in the regions he controls, with all kinds of weapons and all methods, fighting him everywhere at every opportunity. Therefore, guerrilla war has developed its immense strategic effect in wearing out, annihilating, and dispersing the enemy forces to a high degree, in disturbing his strategic arrangement, in creating a strategic position that is favorable to us, and in protecting and training the revolutionary masses.

In our country, guerrilla warfare not only has an important effect in military strategy, it also has very great significance in fulfilling the strategic task of the revolution. Guerrilla warfare is a formula of the revolutionary masses for carrying out insurrection stage by stage and for seizing back the basic administrative power for the people.

At the beginning of a national liberation war, when the people in revolt rise up to carry out insurrection stage by stage, and when they have only small armed forces, they can only wage guerrilla warfare. To maintain their offensive impetus and defeat the enemy's counterattack, they must tirelessly carry out guerrilla war and partial insurrection. From regional armed forces, they must build increasingly stronger main-force troops and must incessantly develop guerrilla war into regular war. Only through regular war, in which the main-force troops fight in a concentrated manner and the armed services are combined, and only through fighting in coordination with regional troops, militia guerrillas, and the political forces of all the people, can the revolutionaries annihilate important forces of the enemy, liberate vast areas of land, score increasingly greater victories, and create conditions for making great strides in the war.

In our country's revolutionary war, guerrilla war is the base of regular war. That is why, after the emergence of regular war, it must be closely coordinated with guerrilla war in order to defeat all the enemy's offensive and counteroffensive efforts and create conditions for consolidating and developing guerrilla war. Only where guerrilla war grows and thrives does regular war find favorable conditions for developing powerfully and moving incessantly forward.

When the three categories of troops coordinate closely among themselves, and when the two forms of war assist each other, help each other develop, and are coordinated with the political struggle and other facets of struggle, they will bring about the powerful development of the great force of people's war. In the long-term revolutionary war, guerrilla war must advance to the regular-war stage, and these two forms of war must be closely coordinated. This is the law for achieving victory in people's war in our country.

The big question in directing the war is to know how to transform guerrilla war into regular war at the correct time and correct place, and how to coordinate guerrilla warfare with regular warfare closely and appropriately in each stage and on each battlefield, so that they grow without interruption and develop their increasingly great strategic effects.

Should the enemy recklessly unleash an aggressive war with his ground forces against the northern part of our country, regular war and guerrilla war—assuming the full development of the three troop categories—would appear simultaneously and at the very beginning, closely coordinating with each other.

(2) So that all forces of war will develop their greatest strength, we must seek to build the strategic position of people's war. The development of guerilla and regular warfare along with the development of political struggle and armed insurrection will create favorable conditions for building a strategic position favorable to us and unfavorable to the enemy. To build a strategic position of people's war that is favorable to us and holds the enemy in an unfavorable strategic situation is a very important part of the military art.

In warfare, the strategic force of each participant needs appropriate expansion in order to be able to develop its strength. Imperialism, which wages an aggressive war, relies on its regular army with many weapons, modern technical means, and maintenance of a large organizational network. To develop its great strength, this force must be expanded according to the theory that a battle position must have a front line. To wage a revolutionary war, we rely on the force of the entire country, using the people's armed forces as a core, while fighting the bandits right on our territory. By organizing all the people to fight the bandits, we have created a strategy that encircles and attacks the enemy politically and militarily directly in the areas under his temporary occupation.

By coordinating political struggle with armed struggle, armed insurrection with revolutionary war, guerrilla war with regular war, and by coordinating the fight against the enemy in the three strategic zones, we have created a fresh, [diverse?] strategic situation in which the enemy's modern army is split up, encircled and everywhere attacked from four directions, thus making it impossible for him to find any area that he can call safe in a war where there is no front, no rear, and no definite front line, and where any place can become a battle-field.

Submerged in the great ocean of people's war, the enemy finds that his eyes and ears are covered. He fights without seeing his opponent, he strikes without hitting, and he is unable to make effective use of his strong combat methods. For this reason, even though the enemy has many troops and much equipment, his forces are scattered, weakened, and unable to develop their efficiency as he wants. Our armed and political forces, however, can constantly encircle the enemy and rise up to fight him everywhere.

Under such circumstances, our forces can develop their powerful effect, always hold the initiative in striking at the enemy, fight him anywhere, at any time, and at their own choosing, hit him each time they strike, and wipe him out in increasingly greater numbers.

In such a strategic situation, even though the enemy has many troops and much modern equipment, he cannot put up a solid defense everywhere. His scattered and passive strategic position will always show many weak spots and exposed areas.

Our armed forces can take advantage of their own favorable strategic position and use appropriate forces to deal unexpected, dangerous, and painful blows to him.

In the course of the development of our armed and political forces, the three troop categories will gradually grow on all battlefields. To defeat an enemy with high mobility, we must create the right strategic position for the three [categories of forces]—the main-force troops, the regional armed forces, and the political forces that have developed in vital strategic areas and that are closely coordinated among themselves. In this strategic position, we may be able actively to deal the enemy powerful combined blows in important areas. As for the enemy, wherever he goes he will be counterattacked by us. Despite his modern equipment, the enemy will still be unable to move as fast and be as combat ready as our local forces. Because of this, when U.S. troops carried out a mass invasion of our country in 1965, our armed forces and people immediately attacked them everywhere and, firmly maintaining and developing an offensive strategy, caused them great losses and successively defeated their two dry-season counteroffensives.

In war, only when we have strong forces organized in an appropriate manner and with high combat quality, can we annihilate the enemy. When we have strong and well-trained forces, and when we are able to create a favorable position in strategy as well as in campaign and combat, we will be able to develop to a high degree the combat efficiency of our forces, to use a small force to defeat a larger one, to create a great fighting strength from a small force, and constantly to fight the enemy on our own initiative and annihilate him from a position of strength.

Conversely, because he is held in a unfavorable strategic position, the enemy can use only a small part of his troops despite his large army, cannot hit his opponent despite his strong firepower, and can display only poor mobility despite his large capability in this field. Although he has great strength, he cannot develop its effect. Although he is extremely belligerent and perfidious, he is always passive and on the receiving end of our blows. In other words, although he is numerous, he is outnumbered; although he is strong, he is weak.

(3) The question of determining correctly the direction of an opportunity for attack is an important question in military art. From the practice of insurrection and revolutionary war, we can see that if we attack from one direction with a certain force, we may be able to wipe out a certain enemy force, but this will not greatly influence the general situation and the victory achieved is only at the campaign and tactical level. On the other hand, if we attack from another direction, we can deal a formidable blow to the enemy and gain a victory of strategic importance.

Looking back at the course of our people's armed struggle, we can see many examples of success in insurrection and war from correctly determining the direction of attack. Clearly the choice of direction of attack is, strategically, a very big question of military art.

Parallel with the art of choosing the direction of attack is choosing the opportunity for attack. It has a decisive importance in insurrection and is also very important in war. By seizing the correct opportunity, we may be able to attack the enemy while his forces are still scattered, when he is not on guard, or when he is in a confused state thus making it impossible for him to cope with us, rendering him vulnerable to annihilation, and enabling us to score great victories.

(4) In war, the choice of appropriate forms of warfare and the proper organization of armed forces and their use in response to the requirements of these forms are an important problem in military art. In leading armed struggle and establishing a strategy, our Party has always paid attention to the forms of warfare and to a military organization that is appropriate to the actual development of our armed forces, considering the relative strength of the enemy and ourselves and other strategic conditions of each stage.

In preparing for the August Revolution and to carry out the strategy of guerrilla war, our Party drew up the form of guerrilla warfare to include such tactics as turning a disadvantageous position into an advantageous one—ambush, hitting from the rear, and so forth—and such forms of organizing as secret armed cells, guerrilla cells, and guerrilla squads.

During the early years of the resistance against the French colonialists, the strategy of starting and stepping up guerrilla warfare behind enemy lines was carried out by various forms of armed propaganda and by the guerrilla activities of various types of organizations: armed propaganda squads, independent companies, and [heavily armed?] battalions. These guerrilla activities gradually developed into small guerrilla operations behind enemy lines, with the participation of main-force regiments and in cooperation with local armed forces.

Later, substantial military operations were launched employing such styles of warfare as attacks and guerrilla activities against mobile forces or fortified positions. To respond to these types of warfare, the main forces were organized into brigades, the cores of which were infantry combined with technicians.

In the present war of liberation in South Vietnam, our armed forces and people, in their process of stepping up warfare and insurrection, have used varied and efficient formulas of warfare appropriate to realities of the battlefield. As the war has developed, various kinds of military operations with new content have been applied in each stage. Military operations by guerrillas and main forces, combined with local armed forces and political forces from the masses, have been launched against every enemy strategic position. Along with these forms of warfare, the organization and use of armed forces are appropriate.

In the north, the air-defense forces' creative forms of warfare, from the three kinds of people's armed forces and the proper organization and use of forces, have contributed an important part to our victory over the U.S. war of destruction. The realities of the way our people conduct war prove that only proper forms of warfare and appropriate organization and use of forces can achieve good results in strategic plans.

By mapping out an appropriate form of warfare in time, we can boost our armed forces' capability in attacking and destroying the enemy and thus step up the war. With a good style of warfare, well applied on the battlefield, our armed forces can [certainly] destroy a large number of enemy, defeat his methods of warfare and his tactics, and thereby defeat his strategic plans.

An important requirement in military art is a skillful combination of styles of warfare that will respond properly to the concrete situation of a given place and time. Each style of warfare must be adapted to the balance of forces between the enemy and ourselves and to the strategic situation of each phase of the war.

Therefore, we must pay attention to the development of these styles so that they can respond to the requirements of each period. When necessary, we must in time change outdated forms of warfare and take up new ones that are more appropriate. Because of this, the organizations that carry out our military operations and attacks have always been developed from war. We must know how to apply past experience [with the aim of better development] and always consider the practical aspects on the battlefield, so that we can constantly improve our strategic, operative, and tactical guidance. We should not apply old experiences mechanically or reapply outmoded forms of warfare.

Along with mapping out styles of warfare, we must also solve the problem of the proper organization and use of forces. Only by constantly attending to improving organizational method in order to respond to the needs of various styles of warfare can we have a basis for organizing proper implementation of these styles of warfare on the battlefield.

Under present circumstances, our armed forces' and people's level of political consciousness is increasingly rising, and our armed forces' equipment is constantly being built up. Therefore, our forms of warfare, as well as our organizational methods and ways of using our forces, are becoming increasingly more numerous. Forms of warfare combining various branches of services are also becoming increasingly effective.

Attention must be paid to the good guidance of organizational method and use of forces, in order to develop fully the role of various branches of services and units, as well as all kinds of troops in the armed forces, in response to rising demands for combined operations by various branches of services and troops.

(5) On the basis of a correct assessment and an intelligent application of the above points, our armed forces and people have solved the problem of raising the combat efficiency of all our armed forces. This is also a factor in our people's military art.

Analyzing past wars, we note that the imperialist aggressors in Vietnam have mobilized great war machines that could not accomplish their strategic tasks, and so, in the end, were defeated by our armed forces and people.

Our enemies have often positioned a large force on the battlefield that could not destroy our force or achieve the objectives of their military operations. On the contrary, our army and people—under various circumstances and with a force of a certain size—can defeat a larger and better-equipped enemy force, destroy the opponent's force, frustrate his plans, and inflict heavy losses on him.

Realities on the battlefield show that the enemy cannot develop his combat efficiency but that we can fully develop ours. Our armed forces can fully develop their combat efficiency because of the rational organization of our force, the appropriate size of each unit, the favorable conditions we always create under which to attack the enemy, and the superior fighting methods we employ in exploiting our strong points and his weak points in order to destroy him.

We have also prevented the enemy from developing his combat efficiency by holding the combat initiative with our skillful, secret, and sudden attacks.

Thus, whenever we launch an attack, we hit right on target

and destroy the enemy, whereas the enemy cannot hit the right target in order to destroy us. He has a huge force but can develop little efficiency.

Assessing the combat efficiency of troops does not necessarily mean looking at the results of each engagement. In general, in every battle we must use our force rationally and employ superior fighting methods, so that we can destroy many enemy troops but suffer ourselves as little as possible.

However, sometimes in war there are important battles whose difficulties, whatever they may be, we must be determined to overcome at all costs to destroy the enemy. Victory in these battles will create favorable conditions for the success of the entire campaign. In these cases, considering the entire campaign, the important victorious battles are those revealing a high combat efficiency.

The above points are also drawn from the history of our people's military art for national defense. Fighting small skirmishes in order to grow in strength, engaging in big battles to achieve victory in a protracted war, combining small attacks by local forces with big offensives by regular troops, trying to create favorable conditions for an offensive to weaken and destroy a large enemy force, choosing a right place and time to deal the enemy a decisive blow, using a bold fighting method, and swiftly mobilizing a big force to deal a sudden, decisive blow at the enemy nerve-center to gain a great victory in lightning attacks—these are typical examples of the successes in military art applied Ly Thuong Kiet, Tran Huong Dao, Le Loi, Nguyen Trai, and Nguyen Hue.

In new historical conditions, the military art of people's war has developed to a new level. Because of the military knowledge and talent of our people, people's war in our country at present has an invincible strength.

These are the main content, guiding principles, and rules of the formulas for waging war and of the military art of people's war in Vietnam, which have been drawn from the realities of war during past decades.

These contents are closely related and combined into an inseparable system. It is necessary to stress that these are mainly experiences of armed uprisings and revolutionary wars, that is, wars of national liberation to gain power and national independence.

War is a most violent clash of force, a most violent competition in strength and efforts between two sides on the basis of certain objective conditions. Our Party's correct war guidance has fully analyzed various objective conditions of war, correctly assessed the strength of the two sides, steadily held [war objectives?], successfully applied our formulas for waging wars and our military art, and exploited decisive factors in defeating wars of aggression by three imperialist countries.

In war, a most fundamental problem is correctly assessing the enemy's and one's own strength. A strong point in our Party's war guidance is the correct and scientific assessment of the balance of forces between the enemy and ourselves. This assessment must be total and substantial, not only on the military side but also on the political front, not only quantitatively but also qualitatively, taking in not only troop strength but also the strength of the people's revolution. Seeing not only the enemy's strong points and our side's weak points but also all our strong points and all his weak points.

Assessment of the two sides' war-waging capability involves comparing not only sheer force but also position, not only real strength and position of the two sides but also the enemy's combat efficiency and our own, and the two sides' strength not only throughout the country but also on each battlefield. We must also compare the strength of the enemy and ourselves in the world and in contemporary times. Only by such a total comparison can we correctly assess our own and the enemy's capability and potential on the battlefield.

This comparison of strength must also be based on dialectical viewpoints, seeing all developments and changes in our situation and that of the enemy.

In addition to comparing strength and position between the two sides, the most important point is: a correct assessment of the role of the enemy's leadership and ours, and a comparison of the great effects of our correct line and the enemy's false line, and of our superior [military] art and the enemy's reactionary and outmoded art. On the basis of a correct and objective assessment of the relative strength of the enemy and ourselves, our Party has led our people to rise up and fight the enemy, has developed its outstanding ability in conducting the war to defeat the enemy, and has led people's war in the right direction to complete victory.

In the wars waged on our soil, we and the enemy have relied on different forces. Both sides have different strong and weak points, different fighting methods, and different strategic viewpoints. Each side has attempted to develop its strength and strong points to defeat the opponent.

The outstanding point in our military art has been the knowledge of how to develop our strength and advantageous fighting methods, and how to prevent the enemy from developing his strength and strong points. We use our strong points to fight his weak points, continually destroying the enemy's force and his strategic plans on an increasing scale to defeat him completely.

Helpless before the superior military line and correct and creative war guidance of our Party, and confronted by our people's great strength, the enemy wants to have a swift, decisive fight but has to face a protracted war. The enemy wants to create a war with definite front lines but has to accept one without front lines. He wants to concentrate his forces but has to scatter them. He wants to retain the combat initiative to develop his strength and strong points but is forced into a passive position in facing our strength and advantageous fighting methods. He wants to launch attacks but is placed in a defensive position. He wants to destroy our force, but his force is destroyed by us. He wants to use his strength to destroy our potentials, but his potential is greatly reduced. His strategies have gone bankrupt one after another. The more he has tried to exert great effort the heavier his defeats; and he exerts ever greater effort only to have more disastrous results, and so on to his final defeat.

Thus, a big country with a large, aggressive force equipped with ultramodern weapons can be rendered impotent and be completely defeated by a small nation with courageous and intelligent people who are determined to fight, and who know how to fight.

The defeats on the battlefield are accompanied by the bankruptcy of the U.S. imperialists' outmoded belief that a large force, modern equipment, and a strong air force could achieve victory, and the dissipation of the myth about the unsurpassable strength of U.S. troops.

With the above formulas for waging war and military art, and their proper application according to different conditions, the heroic Vietnamese people have continually achieved great victories in implementing brilliantly the wise thoughts of [Marx and Engels] presented 120 years ago.

A nation that wants to gain independence must not restrict itself to conventional formulas for waging war. The only effective formula is to have uprisings by the masses, revolutionary war, and guerrilla bands operating everywhere. A small nation can defeat a big country and a moderately armed force can resist a strong army with better equipment.

PART 7. *Party Leadership Is the Main Factor Deciding the Victories of the Uprising of All the People and the People's War.*

Praising our Party's extremely glorious process of leading the revolution, President Ho said: "Right after its birth, the Party organized and led the very heroic struggle of the Nghe-Tinh Soviet; at age twelve, it organized the guerrilla movement that fought the French and the Japanese; at age fifteen, it staged and led the successful August Revolution; and at age seventeen, it led the resistance war, which it won at age twenty-four." Our people are now waging the anti-U.S., national salvation resistance war, the greatest war of resistance in our national history. Experience gained from our country's history of national liberation struggles over more than 100 years has demonstrated that, in our time, national liberation wars, revolutionary wars of a true people's nature, can be launched on a uniform basis and can achieve complete victory under the leadership of the Party and working class. Our Party's leadership is the essential condition and the main factor determining the success of the uprising of all the people and people's war in our country, paving the way toward socialism, and preserving the fruit of the socialist revolution. This is because our party is the Vietnam workers' new-style Party; it has a thoroughly revolutionary spirit, a scientific Marxist-Leninist theory, a strict and disciplined organization, and close relations with the masses. Our Party's emergence resulted from a combination of Marxism-Leninism with the workers' movement and the Vietnamese national liberation movement. Ever since its birth, our Party has assumed sole leadership over the revolution in our country. It is the Party of the working class and of the Vietnamese people as well.

Today, only the Workers' Party*—the most resolutely revolutionary class representing the socialist solution formula,

* The Lao Dong (Communist Party).—ED.

the basic interests of the masses, the large ranks of workers and laborers, and the basic and long-range interests of our people—can be our people's legitimate leader, can hoist high the national and democratic banner, can lead the national democratic revolution toward complete success and the country toward socialism, and can mobilize and lead our people in arising and pursuing the revolutionary war until victory. Only our Party can have revolutionary courage [words indistinct] mobilize the masses to stand up to attack with their bare hands the colonialist and feudalistic imperialists' ruling yoke, to overcome every difficulty and hardship, and to defeat the cruel and powerful aggressor imperialists, including the U.S. imperialists—the ringleader imperialists and the number-one enemy of the people of the world.

Fulfilling revolutionary tasks at all costs, our Party has become a Party experienced in leading the uprising of all the people and people's war. It possesses correct and creative revolutionary lines. It has firmly grasped the laws governing the revolution and the revolutionary war, and it has exercised resolute, bold, and scientific leadership over the implementation of political and military lines. The Party has closely associated itself with the masses, forming a steadfast nucleus for the great unity block of all the people.

As a result, the party has further mobilized large and strong forces throughout the country to unite closely around it, to overcome every challenge, and to lead the revolutionary offensive toward victory. The Party's leadership of the uprising of all the people and people's war has been reflected primarily in the way it determines the correct political and military lines, sets forth the tasks and the basic and urgent goals of the revolution, and determines and leads the implementation of revolutionary methods, the forms for organizing forces, the methods and tricks involved in the struggle, and the most appropriate, sharpest, and most effective and revolutionary combat methods, as mentioned above.

Party leadership is also demonstrated by the following points:

First: To carry out continuously and vigorously political motivation among all the Party, army, and people, to cultivate and develop highly Vietnamese revolutionary heros, to cultivate the spirit of determination to fight and win, to build supreme political and moral strength in order to defeat the enemy, and to achieve by every means the revolutionary objectives and the objectives set forth for each period.

Lenin said that, in the final analysis, victory in any war is determined by the willingness of the masses to shed blood on the battlefield. The masses' awareness of the cause and objectives of the war is of very great significance and is a guarantee of victory.

While leading the people's war, our Party, complying with Lenin's teaching, has constantly given top priority to educating the masses regarding the war line and the revolutionary tasks and political objectives of the war, constantly motivating the masses politically, and intensifying the political and moral factors of the revolutionary war. The political and moral strength of the war is determined primarily by the revolutionary line and the political objectives of the war. The Party's revolutionary line and the political objectives of revolutionary war reflect the law governing the development of history. They also reflect our people's profound aspirations, primarily those of the masses of workers and laborers. Once this line has deeply permeated the masses, it is translated into an intense revolutionary determination of will and into an extremely great motivational force underlying the revolutionary war.

In the war, our Party has persistently and systematically educated Party members, the army, and the people regarding the revolutionary line and tasks, the objectives of the war, the correct assessment of the balance of forces and the development trends existing between us and the enemy, and the protracted, arduous, yet inevitably victorious character of the revolutionary war. Our Party has constantly intensified political education and strengthened ideological leadership in the army and among the people, educating them regarding the sense of class and national consciousness, intensifying their love for the country and for the new system—the people's democratic and socialist system—and enhancing their proletarian, internationalist spirit.

Our Party has disseminated among the masses President Ho's great principle, "Nothing is more precious than independence and freedom," and the determined-to-fight spirit, "Prefer to sacrifice everything rather than let the country be lost and serve as slaves."

Developing the determined-to-fight-and-win spirit and the spirit of sacrifice for national salvation, our Party has constantly conducted an ideological struggle against erroneous tendencies, especially those of rightist thought and fear of a protracted war, hardship, and so forth.

One of our Party's great successes has been to improve Vietnamese revolutionary heroism and collective heroism, which have been highly developed and have become new ethics and fine qualities that have spread among millions of people and combatants, from the front line to the rear, in all combat positions, and in all aspects of the revolutionary struggle.

Vietnamese revolutionary heroism is the crystallization of the working-class revolutionary character and our people's fine virtues:

It is the high spirit of heroically and courageously making sacrifices and of not shrinking before any enemy authority or any difficulty or danger. In coordination with intelligence and resourcefulness, it creates revolutionary methods and tricks to defeat the enemy in all aspects of struggle. It is reflected concisely in President Ho's commendations to our people's armed forces and our heroic people: "Fulfill any task, overcome any difficulty, and defeat any enemy."

Vietnamese revolutionary heroism is our people's will and determination to win independence and freedom and to protect the results in all fields of the revolution, results that they have won under Party leadership.

Our people, after enduring countless suffering and misfortunes under the old regime, have enjoyed an independent and free life under the new regime. Therefore, our people have all the more resolutely fought to the end to gain and protect independence and freedom. Vietnamese revolutionary heroism is the synthesis of the deep education and daily training in various aspects of consciousness with regard to revolutionary ideology, intellect, and feelings. This constitutes a strong manifestation of enlightenment regarding revolutionary tasks, the war goal, strong patriotism, profound hatred for the enemy, the determination to fight and win, and absolute confidence in our Party, President Ho, the people's strength and heroic tradition, class, and the combat ability of the community and of every individual. Vietnamese revolutionary heroism is the great spiritual force of our people, our nation, and the Vietnamese people in the new era and the new social regime. We fought fiercely for national liberation, for the protection of the fatherland, and for national protection and construction.

The formula for prosecuting the war and the heroic and intelligent military art of our party have been built, shaped up, and developed from the realities of the great struggle conducted by millions of Vietnamese people displaying revolutionary heroism. Only by relying on and highly developing Vietnamese revolutionary heroism can the Party's formula for prosecuting the war and its military art result in revolutionary action by the masses and bring about practical successes in the war. The marvelous feats of arms of our army and people, from the front line to the rear base area, have been so far the feats of arms of Vietnamese revolutionary heroism and our Party's great achievement in political mobilization and ideological formation and in building the new Vietnamese people.

Second: To mobilize fully the potentialities of people's war while stepping up the prosecution of the war, gradually fulfilling revolutionary tasks, strengthening the victorious elements of the war, and insuring the leading of the war toward final victory.

Lenin said that "whichever has more reserves and human resources and whoever can stand more firmly among the masses and people than others will win victory in a war." In our national liberation war, we have attacked vigorously and won great victories, and we have defeated large enemy forces with small forces.

In order to win victory, we must know how to acquire greater strength than the enemy and how to use the forces of our entire people and country to defeat the imperialists' large, aggressive armed forces in our country. Therefore, on the basis of politically mobilizing all our people, our Party has paid special attention to mobilizing fully the potentialities of the people's war and to strengthening the victorious factors of the war. During the previous, anti-French resistance, President Ho pointed out: "The victorious key task of the resistance consists of consolidating and broadening the united national front, of consolidating the worker-peasant alliance, of consolidating the Party and strengthening its leadership in all fields." In the present anti-U.S. resistance, President Ho also pointed out: "Our lines and policies are correct, our entire people are united and single-minded, and our armed forces are matchlessly heroic. We are also wholeheartedly aided by the fraternal countries in the socialist camp and greatly supported by friends world-wide. Therefore, we will certainly win, and the Americans will certainly be defeated." This is the comprehensive, adequate recapitulation of the factors and conditions that insure the victory of the people's war, the revolutionary war in our country in the present era.

In the process of war, our Party has endeavored to build and improve comprehensively and systematically these factors and conditions of success, thus creating a national force as great as possible and obtaining broad and active support from the people of the world in defeating the enemy.

A very basic matter involved in this objective is that our Party has always grasped and correctly settled the relation between stepping up the revolutionary war and carrying out step-by-step revolutionary tasks in the process of war. It has asserted that the Party-directed revolutionary war is a means [words indistinct] of guaranteeing the implementation of the revolution's strategic missions, in case the imperialist invader used counterrevolutionary war to oppose our people's revolutionary war, and of carrying it on until victory. Thus, [only by?] overthrowing the ruling yoke of the imperialists and their lackeys can we achieve the basic objective of the revolution.

On the other hand, to strengthen the force of the revolutionary war and improve the chances of success and the force of war in all respects, our Party has relied on existing circumstances to lead the people to carry out, step by step, revolutionary tasks in the midst of the process of war. This is precisely the question of grasping the relation between revolution and revolutionary war in the process of directing and guiding the war.

During the anti-French resistance war, our Party set forth the policy of simultaneously fighting three enemies: famine, illiteracy, and foreign aggression. In order to improve the people's strength during the resistance war, especially that of the peasants, the greatest force of the resistance, our Party led them to carry out democratic reforms, gradually implement its land-reform plan, and advance toward motivating the masses to reduce land rent thoroughly and realize land reform. This is a correct and inventive policy of our Party.

In the north, in the present anti-U.S., national salvation resistance war, our Party has advocated simultaneously carrying on the resistance and continuing to accelerate the building of socialism while changing the direction of the construction of the economy according to war conditions, with a view to strengthening the economic and national defense potential of the north, stabilizing the people's life, and developing the comprehensive superiority of socialism, so as to defeat the enemy in the people's war against his war of destruction and to fulfill the duty of the great rear base area toward the great front line. This is another correct and inventive policy of our Party.

In the liberated areas in the south, under the leadership of the NLF and the Provisional Revolutionary Government of the Republic of South Vietnam, our people have fought bravely while regaining and preserving revolutionary achievements and building a new political, economic, and cultural life directed by the people. These policies of our Party have established steady economic and political bases for improving the people's strength comprehensively during the resistance war, consolidating the worker-peasant alliance—an alliance between the working class and agricultural laborers in a national democratic revolution, and between the working class and the class of collective peasants in a socialist revolution—the people's administration, and the united national front, heightening the fighting strength of the people's armed forces, and consolidating and strengthening the Party's leadership.

In wartime, coordination between accelerating the resistance and carrying out step-by-step revolutionary tasks also means coordination between intensifying the front line and consolidating the rear base area, between fighting the enemy and building and improving our forces so that they will always be strong when they fight. The gradual implementation of revolutionary tasks in wartime is also a very basic way to improve and develop the masses' great political and spiritual strength and to develop highly Vietnamese heroism [on] the firm basis of the new production formula of the new social regime ruled by the people.

Third: To build and consolidate the Party's leadership system, from central to local organs, among the people's armed forces and among all other masses' organizations, and in the military, political, economic, and cultural struggle realms, in order to insure the Party's comprehensive, concentrated, and united leadership in wartime.

The Party's leadership is the decisive factor for success in the war. This is true and necessary not only vis-à-vis the whole war but also vis-à-vis each locality and aspect of the struggle. Our revolutionary war attacks the enemy with the combined strength of all revolutionary means and every other means to fight the enemy everywhere, while building forces in every aspect. Therefore, in a long process of struggle, our

Party must build and improve its leadership system, from central to local organs, among the people's armed forces and all forces, on the military front and in all other aspects of struggle, according to the lines, "the Party's leadership is where the masses' struggles are" and "insure the Party's comprehensive, concentrated and united leadership" requirements.

Our Party has built and consolidated its leadership system, from central to local organs, from the Party Central Committee to Party echelons on battlefields and in provinces, districts, and villages. From the army's Central Military Affairs Party Committee to company Party chapters, Party organs have always been present in the army.

Moreover, our Party set forth four relationships between its army organs and local leading organs, thus insuring the Party's concentrated and united leadership vis-à-vis all the forces and regional as well as nationwide struggle.

In rural areas, the village is the fundamental unit of people's war. The village Party chapter and Party echelon constitute the staff of people's war in villages. In the anti-French resistance, as well as in the present anti-U.S. resistance, we made each village a bunker and each village Party echelon and chapter a staff of people's war. The village Party chapter has led the people in building combat villages, developing guerrilla warfare, strongly stepping up the political struggle, safeguarding the people, regaining and maintaining local administrative power, and in coordinating their combat with that of main-force troops; it has also led the people in developing production, building a new life, consolidating the rear, and providing the front with manpower and supplies.

All the Party Central Committee's wartime lines and policies have been carried out in villages. Without resolute and active leadership of the local Party chapters, we would never have a strong and persistent national resistance against aggression. To direct the people's war, each echelon's leadership must be comprehensive, encompassing all aspects of the struggle that are essentially military and political, as well as the military and enemy recruitment struggles. It also must build strength in all aspects—military, political, as well as economic—along with consolidating the people's rule while fighting.

The long war has made it necessary for our Party to have a well-formed organization. Each of the Party's leading ranks has much experience in organizing leading organs to struggle and build—organs that materialize the Party's comprehensive, concentrated, and united leadership vis-à-vis people's war as a whole. This is the key condition for creating an efficient, synthesized strength for leading the people's war in each locality.

Since the August Revolution's success, our Party has become the ruling Party. The people's administration, led by our Party, is our Party's and people's important and unique tool for organizing and carrying on the revolutionary war.

Our Party has unceasingly strengthened the leadership of the people's armed forces, the people's administration, and the united national front from central to regional echelons; it has developed to the utmost the functions and resources of these organizations under the united and centralized leadership of the Party. Only by so doing could we satisfactorily ensure the mobilization and organization of the strength of all our nation and people to fight the enemy.

To strengthen Party leadership in the war, it is necessary to step up the building of the Party and training and improvement of cadres and Party members, and to constantly strengthen and improve the *chi bo*'s. The cadres and Party members have the duty to propagandize, educate, and organize the masses to carry on the Party's lines and policies in the war. Therefore, the training and improvement of cadres and Party members is a key problem in understanding the Party's leadership in the war and an important point in the Party-building task. It is necessary constantly to have a strong —both quantitatively and qualitatively—cadre organization to meet the requirements of the leadership task in the development of the war.

It is necessary to develop the strength of new Party members, to consolidate leadership strength everywhere, and to guide the masses in the struggle to win victories on every battlefield. In the training and improvement of cadres and Party members, primary consideration must be given to the improvement of the class and vanguard character of cadres and Party members. In the war, cadres and Party members must have the sound stand and ideology of the working class and Marxism-Leninism, patriotism, revolutionary eagerness, a stanch fighting spirit for the sake of national liberation and Communism, and a will to forge ahead in the class struggle and the violent struggle of our people.

For scores of years, our cadres and Party members have held high their heroic fighting spirit under every circumstance, attracting the affection and confidence of the people. Many of our cadres and Party members have heroically sacrificed themselves for the fatherland's independence and freedom, for socialism, and for the revolutionary enterprise of our Party and people. This is a source of pride and an honor for our Party. To fulfill the task of wartime leadership, the cadres and Party members must be capable of leading the masses in the military struggle and in other fields of activities in the comprehensive war of all the people. Military training has become an urgent problem for army cadres and Party members as well as for other cadres and Party members.

In preparing for an armed uprising, the Party Central Committee has called on cadres and Party members to undertake military training actively. In the anti-French resistance, when the war had entered a violent and decisive phase, the Second Party Congress convened in 1951 [high-point?] issued a resolution on military training of the Party,* and on direction of the activities of all branches serving the resistance.†

In the present anti-U.S. resistance, our cadres and Party members have rapidly matured, benefiting from numerous experiences on the military front and having many opportunities to carry out their tasks, thus ensuring communications and transportation, economic building, and cultural, educational,

* Second Party Congress document.—GIAP
† Third Party Congess document.—GIAP

and public-health development under the harsh circumstances
of war.

The contingent of cadres and Party members trained in this
protracted war constitutes very valuable capital for our Party
in leading the war to final victory and constantly accelerating
the revolution. As the cells of the Party and as part of the
masses, Party branches must connect the Party with the
masses and lead them in accelerating the revolutionary war in
base areas and stalwartly and resourcefully to struggle against
the enemy on all fronts, every day and every hour, under very
difficult circumstances.

It is necessary to improve the work of Party branches, to set
up strong Party branches in the army, localities, and rural and
urban areas, from the front line to the rear, in the enemy lairs,
and in heavily embattled areas, and to strengthen them so they
can lead the masses in base areas and reinforce Party leadership in war. A Party branch is a major nucleus of resistance in
base areas. Without strong, stalwart, and skillful Party
branches, people's war cannot develop strongly and widely
on all fronts. Local Party branches in the army must constantly hold aloft the banner of the Party's leadership, stand
firm under every circumstance, skillfully direct combat and
other struggles, and achieve comprehensive, concentrated, and
unified leadership in localities as well as in army units.

It is necessary to consolidate and improve Party branches
in every respect; to pay major attention to the link between
educating and developing Party committees; to improve the
leadership task of Party branches; to coordinate closely the
task of consolidating and perfecting Party branches with the
task of leading localities and army units to struggle successfully and to carry out other tasks satisfactorily; to consider as
a goal the fulfillment of the leadership task of Party branches
in war; and to consolidate and perfect Party branches through
the completion of this task.

During scores of years of our Party's resolute struggle,
many stalwart Party branches emerged worthy to be steel

bastions, leading banners, and solid nuclei of people's war at bases, in localities, in many army units, on the front line, in the rear base area, in combat, and in serving the combat forces. Our people's heroic, resourceful struggle has tempered and trained determined, able Party branches for our Party.

Through practical experience and with their warm revolutionary sentiments and reason, our people have demonstrated their absolute confidence in our Party. Our people are very proud of our Party and of our great leader Ho Chi Minh. Our Party is closely connected with the masses. Our people are closely united around our Party and remain its faithful followers.

Only our Party can correctly combine class interests with national interests, the class factor with the national factor, and genuine patriotism with lofty international proletarianism. Only it can carry on our glorious national traditions and open the way for our people's advance toward a brilliant future. Only our Party can mobilize the greatest strength of the nation and win the greatest support from the world revolution to defeat the imperialist aggressors. The constant consolidation and strengthening of our Party's leadership are the essential conditions for victory in the uprising of all the people and people's war.

Fourth: "Nothing is more precious than independence and freedom; hold high President Ho's glorious banner, and bravely advance toward defeating completely the U.S. aggressors."

The past dozen years represent but a short period of time in national history, but, during this short period, under the Party's leadership, our people, our nation, have won repeated great successes. The face of our country and our nation has changed completely. The era of independence, freedom, and socialism for our country has begun. The Ho Chi Minh epoch, the nation's most glorious epoch, has been inaugurated. Our people's successes have all resulted from the Party's stalwart and clear-sighted leadership and correct political and military lines, associated with the name of President Ho, the founder, trainer, and leader of our Party and the beloved father of our people's armed forces.

President Ho was a great leader of the working class and of our nation, a talented strategist, a national hero, and an outstanding combatant in the international Communist movement and the national liberation movement of this century. He was a noble symbol of the perfect combination of genuine patriotism and international proletarianism.* President Ho was the first Communist to apply Marxism-Leninism to actual conditions in our country, setting forth a revolutionary line filled with an independent, self-governing, valiant, and inventive spirit and helping our people to move steadily forward.

We are extremely proud of our Party's and President Ho's revolutionary line, a people's democratic national revolutionary line, a socialist revolutionary line, the people's war line in our country, and a correct international line. Along this line, our country's revolutionary undertaking will continue to advance steadily toward complete victory. President Ho was a symbol of the Vietnamese people's stalwart and unsubmissive spirit throughout their 4,000-year history.†

Inspired by the steadfast and devoted revolutionary spirit of the working class, President Ho stated, "Nothing is more precious than independence and freedom. We will sacrifice all rather than lose the country and live as slaves." He also said, "Only socialism and Communism can liberate the oppressed peoples and the workers throughout the world from the yoke of slavery." ‡ This is the truth distilled from the long process of our national struggle toward national liberation. This is the truth of the present era, in which the working class, which is the genuine leader of the national liberation struggle, opens the way toward socialism. This is the indomitable spirit of our nation and our people's unshaken revolutionary determination. President Ho's thought is a vigorous

---

* Party Central Committee's oration read by Comrade Le Duan, Party First Secretary, at the solemn memorial service for President Ho.—GIAP

† *Ibid.*

‡ Ho Chi Minh, *The Path Leading Us to Leninism.*—GIAP

spiritual motivation and encouragement for our people, who have overcome and are overcoming countless hardships and sacrifices and who are determined to gain independence and freedom.

President Ho told us, "Our people's anti-U.S., national, salvation struggle, although it must undergo many more hardships and sacrifices, will certainly be victorious. This is certain." * The anti-U.S., national salvation resistance is the greatest resistance in our national history. This is the fierce confrontation of the forces on the battlefield in our country between the most revolutionary forces and the most reactionary forces of the present era. Our people's successes are also the common successes of the revolutionary forces and progressives throughout the world. Fighting the U.S. aggressors until we achieve complete victory is our people's present sacred national duty and lofty international obligation.

The U.S. imperialists have been seriously defeated and are going downhill. Yet they remain very stubborn in their plot to invade the southern part of our country and in playing their evil role as international policemen. Nixon's policies since his accession to power and, especially, his November 3, 1969, speech have exposed the U.S. imperialists' evil design and stubbornness. Through the policy of Vietnamization of the war, the U.S. ruling clique still continues to seek a military solution from a position of strength, to turn Johnson's war into Nixon's, and to pursue stubbornly its aggressive war. The Nixon Administration continues to plunge deeper and deeper into the military adventure in Vietnam. This is a challenge to our people, to the revolutionary forces, to the peace forces throughout the world, and to American progressives. Our people have repeatedly defeated the U.S. imperialists, from the neo-colonialist ruling policy represented by Ngo Dinh Diem's fascist regime to their typical special war and the strategy of the limited war during the highest U.S. escalation. How can the U.S. imperialists, on the verge of defeat and decline, hope to win victory by continuing to prolong their ag-

* Excerpts from President Ho's testament.—GIAP

gressive war, by carrying out symbolic U.S. troop withdrawals, and by reverting to a modified and patched-up special war?

The U.S. imperialists have committed and are committing many "unpardonable" crimes against our people. They have perpetrated many barbarous massacres of our compatriots, such as in Ba Lang An and Song My, and many other new Oradour and Lidice cases throughout the southern part of our country. They are like the cruel Huns and are the most barbarous fascists in the twentieth century.

With increasing hatred for the land-grabbers and country-settlers, the southern compatriots and the liberation troops on the great heroic front line, under the leadership of the NLF and the Provisional Revolutionary Government of the Republic of South Vietnam, are upholding their determination to fight and frustrate all war schemes of the U.S. imperialists and their lackeys, to achieve, at all costs, independence and freedom, and to advance toward peacefully reunifying the country.

Our entire Party and all our troops and people are resolved to implement our oaths of honor in homage to President Ho's memory: "We will forever carry aloft the banner of national independence, resolved to fight and defeat the U.S. aggressors to liberate the south, to defend the north, and to reunify the country with a view to meeting President Ho's desire. We are determined to defeat completely the U.S. aggressors and successfully build socialism."*

The protracted revolutionary struggle, full of hardship and sacrifices, as well as glorious victories, has forged our people and army. Our people are very heroic. Our country is a heroic one. Our army is a heroic one, and of our Party President Ho said, "With all the modesty of revolutionaries, we still have the right to say that our Party is very great."

The strength of militant solidarity of our people nationwide under President Ho's glorious banner is invincible. All fra-

* Vietnam Workers' Party Central Committee's oration read by Comrade Le Duan, First Secretary, at the solemn memorial service for President Ho.—GIAP

ternal socialist countries and progressives throughout the world are following our people's struggle daily and heartily urging us on. No reactionary power can prevent our people from steadily advancing toward victory.

Thoroughly imbued with President Ho's thought that "nothing is more precious than independence and freedom" and firmly holding to the invincible weapon that is the Party's correct and military line, our people's armed forces uphold revolutionary heroism and the determined spirit to fight and win. Together with all people, they persevere in and accelerate the anti-U.S., national salvation resistance struggle toward complete victory, aiming at building a peaceful, unified, independent, democratic, prosperous, and powerful Vietnam and holding on forever to the beautiful land of the heroic Vietnamese people.

Our people will certainly win! The U.S. imperialists will certainly be defeated!

Appendix: Principal Vietnamese Names Mentioned in the Text

by

GEORGES BOUDAREL

Bach Dang:
North Vietnamese river that flows into Along Bay about twelve miles north of Haiphong

chi bo:
Communist Party cell

Hoang Hoa Tham (alias De Tham):
Famous Vietnamese resistance leader at the beginning of the twentieth century. He was the only one able to maintain an independent territory until 1913, thanks to the support of the peasants, among whom he had grown up. Camped in the forests of the Yen The region north of Hanoi, he escaped all the expeditions sent against him, particularly that of Colonel Gallieni. On several occasions, the French administration was obliged to reach agreements with him, conceding to him the autonomy of certain cantons. In 1909, following a conspiracy organized by Hoang Hoa Tham's men against the Hanoi garrison in 1908, the French army began a serious campaign that dislodged him from his hideout without being able to capture him. De Tham remained in the woods until 1913 when he was killed by an agent of the police.

On March 20, 1951, the People's Army of Vietnam launched an offensive into the region of Mao Khe, near where Hoang Hoa Tham had once been active, and named it after him.

Hung:
A partly legendary dynasty that reigned in the lower valley of the Red River until 258 B.C. The so-called Dongson civilization, known for its bronze drums, flourished under its kings.

Lam Son:
Village in the interior of Thanh Hoa Province where Le Loi was born and where he established his first revolutionary base

112

Le Loi: Wealthy and cultivated landowner born at Lam Son in Than Hoa Province, where he launched an insurrection against the renewed dominance of the Chinese after 1407. With the help of the great scholar Nguyen Trai, he created a center of resistance in that remote region surrounded by mountains. Starting there, he gradually freed the province of Thanh Hoa, then that of Nghe An, establishing his communications by way of the mountains, since the Chinese controlled the coast. In 1426, he was able to launch three armies toward the Red River delta. Welcomed as liberators by the population, they blockaded most of the Ming troops in the capital. The following year, in an ambush in a Chi Lang mountain pass, he decimated a Chinese army that had come to relieve the occupation forces. When the Chinese commander sued for peace, Le Loi took the advice of Nguyen Trai: He offered to supply the garrison with food and transportation if it would return to China. After ten years of resistance, he ascended the throne in 1428 and reigned until 1433. He was the founder of Vietnam's longest dynasty, the Le dynasty (1428–1789).

One of the first local offensives of the People's Army of Vietnam was named for Le Loi. It was launched on January 2, 1949, in the region of Hoa Binh.

Ly: Dynasty that reigned in Vietnam from 1010 until 1225. Devoutly Buddhist, it ordered the construction of numerous pagodas, particularly the Pagoda of the Single Pillar in Hanoi (1049) and the Temple of Literature, which was dedicated to Confucius. The Ly rulers codified laws, organized administration and education, and established the first competitive examinations among the educated for appointment to the bureaucracy (1075).

Ly Bon: Leader of an insurrection against the Chinese occupation, he proclaimed himself emperor in the Red River delta region (A.D. 544–48).

Ly Thuong Kiet:

A strategist who directed several expeditions against Champa in the South. In order to thwart preparations by the Chinese for an invasion, he organized an expedition in 1075 into the South China provinces of Kwangtung and Kwangsi, where he seized several strongholds. In 1077, at Nhu Nguyet, he fought a Chinese army that had penetrated to the Bac Ninh region about twenty miles from Hanoi.

Mai Thuc Loan, called the Black Emperor:

Leader of an insurrection in Nghe An Province in A.D. 722 against the Chinese occupation. He died at an unknown date in the mountains, where he had been forced to take refuge upon the arrival of a Chinese army.

Nghe An (or Ha Tinh) Soviets:

An insurrectionary peasant movement organized in 1930 by the Indochinese Communist Party in Nghe An and Ha Tinh provinces. These areas were among the most active centers of resistance by scholars at the end of the nineteenth century. Following demonstrations in commercial enterprises in Vinh and Ben Thuy on May 1, the movement spread rapidly throughout the rural areas of the two provinces. The first soviet was established in the village of Vo Liet on September 12. Following intervention by the army, the movement began to decline in October and died out during the first months of 1931.

Ngo Quyen:

First emperor of Vietnam, which he freed from the Chinese occupation by sinking an enemy fleet in the Bach Dang. After having planted stakes in the river bed, he pretended to flee in order to induce the enemy to pursue him at high tide and to impale its ships on the stakes at low tide. The stratagem was used again by Tran Huong Dao in the thirteenth century. Ngyo Quyen reigned from A.D. 939 to 944.

Nguyen:

Dynasty founded in 1802 by Prince Nguyen Anh, descendant of the lords who had affirmed their supremacy at Hue since the seventeenth century. The last ruler of the dynasty was the Emperor Bao Dai. Although Nguyen Anh appealed for the help of French officers in order to ascend the throne, Nguyen politics took the form of a return to strict Confucian traditions and the closing of ports of trade. They re-established Chinese as the language of administration and instruction and drew up a law code modeled on that of China's Ch'ing Dynasty (the Gia-long code). The reign of the Nguyen family witnessed the building of the fortifications, palaces, and monumental tombs that make Hue a city of art.

Nguyen Hue:

One of the three Tay Son brothers who headed a peasant revolt in Central Vietnam in 1771. A great commander, he led many brilliant campaigns, as often against Nguyen Anh and the Siamese in the south as against the Trinh in the north. After a forced march, he defeated a Chinese army on the outskirts of Hanoi by gambling on the effect of a surprise attack during the Tet festivities in the winter of 1789. Soon thereafter, he proclaimed himself emperor under the name of Quang Trung. During his very brief reign, he reorganized the administration, increased agricultural production, and encouraged commerce through a policy of opening the ports. He made the national language the language of administration and instruction, which, until then, had only been conducted in classical Chinese. He died suddenly in 1792, and some of the reforms he envisaged have yet to be instituted. The mobility of his troops has remained proverbial.

From May 28 to June 20, 1951, the People's Army of Vietnam unleashed an important offensive that was named after Quang Trung. It was carried out in the Ninh Binh region, through which Quang Trung had marched on Hanoi in 1788–89.

Nguyen Thien Thuat (1844–1926):

Military figure of the mandarin class who took part in engagements against the French army in Tonkin in 1882. He organized a resistance movement in the marshland southeast of Hanoi following the 1885 appeal of the young emperor Ham-nghi. Forced to flee to China, he played an important role in the nationalist emigration of the early nineteenth century. He died in exile near Nanning in Kwangsi Province.

Nguyen Trai (1380–1442):

Great scholar who joined Le Loi at the beginning of his insurrectionary activity against China in 1418 and who served as his military and diplomatic adviser. During the campaign to free the provinces of Than Hoa, Nge An, and Thuan Hoa, his literary talent and political tact brought about the surrender of a number of garrisons. His adroitness made it possible to resolve the delicate problem of getting the Chinese forces to withdraw without offending the Chinese court. In 1442, although he had already been living in retirement for a long time, he and his entire family were condemned to death as the result of a court intrigue.

Strategist and poet, with an encyclopedic and humanist mind, Nguyen Trai is the author of a geography, diplomatic documents, letters and orders to the army in Chinese characters, and a volume of poems in the national language. This last is the oldest Vietnamese literary text that has survived until today. In 1428, in the name of the Emperor Le Loi, he wrote a "Proclamation of Victory over the Chinese" that has remained famous in the history of Vietnam:

> Emperor by the grace of heaven, I proclaim:
>
> We want soldiers in order to set the people free, in order to disarm violence
>
> Our country is the Great Viet
>
> It is an ancient and glorious nation

Nguyen Trung Truc:

Military figure of the mandarin class who continued the struggle against the French after the signing of the 1862 treaty, which ceded eastern Cochin China to France. He led a brief resistance movement in the mountains of the Ha Tien region and the area of Phu Quoc near Cambodia. He surprised the garrison of Rach Gia and destroyed it in 1868. He was captured shortly thereafter and executed. He is said to have declared just before his death: "So long as a blade of grass grows in the earth of the South, there will be men to fight the Westerners."

Phan Dinh Phung: Scholarly winner of the examinations for the bureaucracy. He fulfilled the functions of censor at the court with an exemplary integrity during the reign of the Tu-duc Emperor. Although he had retired to his land in Ha Tinh Province, he responded to the 1885 appeal of the Emperor Ham-nghi to "restore the power of the throne" after Hue had fallen to the French army. He established a fortified camp in the mountains and maintained relations with Siam. Between 1885 and 1895, he led an active resistance movement in Ha Tinh and Nghe An provinces. For the Vietnamese of today, he remains a model of uncompromising patriotism. When a mandarin bureaucrat had the tombs of Phan's parents desecrated in order to draw him back to his village, he told an emissary who sought to remind him of the sacredness of family graves and of his filial duties: "I have only one tomb I must preserve today— the earth of Vietnam."

Thang Long: Former name of Hanoi

Tran Huong Dao: Thirteenth-century strategist who twice repulsed Mongol invasions. In 1284–85, he fought 500,000 men of the armies of Togan, the son of Kubla Khan, who threatened the Red River delta in a pincer movement from the south and the north. With the help of fine commanders, Huong Dao maintained the morale of his troops, although he had to yield key positions during 1284. The next year, he took the offensive when the invaders began to suffer from the combined effects of the climate and his harassment. Defeated at Ham Tu, Chung Zuong, Tay Ket, and Van Kiep, the Mongol armies were completely routed in August, 1284. The offensive against them had lasted about three months.

In 1278, with 300,000 men, Togan again crossed the frontier, while a Mongol navy sailed toward the Vietnamese coast. Again leaving a vacuum in front of the enemy, while constantly harassing his rear lines, Huong Dao took the offensive the moment the Mongol forces began to fall back. Making use of Ngo Quyen's stratagem, his men seized 400 junks in the Bach Dang River. During the summer of 1288, the Vietnamese emperor returned to his capital and throne and quickly dispatched a mission to China to negotiate for peace and offer tribute.

To instruct his troops, Tran Huong Dao drew up an *Outline of Strategy,* inspired by Sun Tzu. In a text entitled *The Secrets of the Battle of Van Kiep*, he formulated this principle: "If one maneuvers cleverly, there is no need for battle orders; if the battle orders are clever, there is no need to fight."

His memory is venerated in the temple of Kiep Bac, a famous center for pilgrims.

The first major offensive of the People's Army toward the Red River delta in the Vinh Yen region on January 16, 1951, was named the "Tran Huong Dao campaign."

Trung: The name of two sisters, Trung Trac and Trung Nhi, who raised an army against the Chinese in A.D. 40–43 and drowned themselves in the river after their defeat in order to avoid capture by the enemy. In Hanoi itself is a temple devoted to their cult.

Trung Cong Dinh: Military figure of the mandarin class who refused to lay down his arms in 1862 in Cochin China, despite the orders of the emperor. He adopted the title "Great Marshal to Pacify the French" and led a resistance movement southeast of Saigon. Repudiated by the court at Hue, he inscribed this motto on his flag: "The court abandons the people." Wounded as the result of a betrayal, he committed suicide in 1864 to avoid being captured.